An 86-mile walking route across some of the Cotswold's most beautiful countryside

ONTENTS

Published by

The Macmillan Way Association,
St Mary's Barn, Pillerton Priors,
Warwick CV35 0PG

First published May 1999

ISBN 0 9526851 1 6

Printed and bound in Great Britain by
The Ancient House Press, Ipswich.

Front Cover Photograph:
Above Whichford - Page 15

Introducing the Cross-Cotswold Pathway

This 86-mile walking route across the Cotswolds from Banbury to Bath is based largely on the Cotswold section of the 290-mile, Coast-to-Coast, Long-Distance Path known as the Macmillan Way. But the Cross-Cotswold's starting and finishing sections have been specially planned to provide walkers with the best possible bus and train links at the northern and southern ends of the Cotswolds - hence the Banbury start and the Bath finish. Like the Macmillan Way itself, the Cross-Cotswold Pathway has been developed to increase public awareness of Macmillan Cancer Relief and to assist in the raising of further funds for this vitally important charitable organisation, whose role is to improve the lives of people with cancer and their families.

In view of this, anyone walking along this path can feel that they are walking '*Across Country for Cancer Care*', as our waymark logo proudly proclaims along the whole course of the route. Like most long-distance paths, the Cross-Cotswold follows existing footpaths, bridleways and byways, and small stretches of minor roads when these are unavoidable. It starts from Banbury Cross, at the centre of this historic town, and heads westwards across the rolling Oxfordshire Cotswolds soon passing lovely Broughton Castle. It then follows the course of a Roman road almost to the village of Epwell, where it joins the Macmillan Way, the course of which will then be followed all the way to Box in Wiltshire.

Banbury Cross - the start of our journey

Beyond Epwell the path turns south-westwards onto Ditchedge Lane, an ancient 'green-road' that runs along the border between Oxfordshire and Warwickshire. At the end of this lane the path drops down into a valley, going across the infant River Stour at mysteriously named 'Traitor's Ford', now firmly in Warwickshire. It next goes through the village of Whichford and through woodlands before climbing up into the true Cotswolds beyond Long Compton. The path now crosses high wold country not far from the prehistoric Rollright Stones and past the National Trust's lovely Chastleton House, before descending into the broad Evenlode Valley, with its memories of Jane Austen and the First World War poet, Edward Thomas. Into Gloucestershire, the path passes the fascinating Oddington Church before climbing once more onto the wolds to go through Maugersbury, with a possible diversion to busy Stow-on-the-Wold.

From Maugersbury our path crosses the Roman's Fosse Way before going over meadows beside the little River Dikler. Soon, ever-popular Lower Slaughter is reached and many walkers will stop here awhile to gaze at its streamside cottages and to visit its interesting little Mill Museum. Now the path climbs a small ridge before descending to the River Windrush and then up again onto classic wold country. It soon goes through Cold Aston and along a lovely 'green-road', known as Bangup Lane, to Turkdean - the second of two typically attractive Cotswold villages. Beyond Turkdean the route heads across more high country before going through Hampnett, where the River Leach has its source on a wide green.

Now the path crosses more rolling country before going through Yanworth, a minute village with a small church, which has a wall painting of Old Father Time on one of its walls. The Cross-Cotswold now drops down into yet another valley, and follows up beside the wooded banks of the River Coln, before passing the National Trust's Chedworth Roman Villa. Beyond here the path climbs up through woodland and eventually goes through the pretty village of Chedworth. It now traverses more high country before crossing the infant River Churn in a wooded valley just beyond the village of Rendcomb (from where it is possible to divert into the bustling market town of Cirencester). Our path now goes through the hamlet of Woodmancote and across a ford in the Dunt Valley in the delightful village of Duntisbourne Rouse, with its tiny Saxon church.

Now skirting the great Cirencester Park, it passes through the village of Sapperton before going through extensive woodlands to emerge close to the east portal of the old Thames and Severn Canal and the nearby source of the River Thames - the start of another Long Distance Path. The Cross-Cotswold Path now heads westwards over slightly flatter wold country, through the hamlets of Tarlton and Hazleton before passing the villages of Cherington and Avening. Beyond the latter it turns southwards across open farmland, passing the lovely Elizabethan manor house of Chavenage before providing an optional diversion into the pleasant market town of Tetbury. It soon heads right through the splendid Westonbirt Arboretum before continuing southwards into quiet Wiltshire farming country.

The attractive village of Sherston, with its wide 'West Country' street and stout church tower, is soon reached and the path follows a small tributary of the Wiltshire Avon to Luckington, which has a delightful house beside its church. From here the path goes across flat farmland to the village of Littleton Drew before passing beneath the noisy M4 motorway. Not far beyond the prehistoric Lugbury Long Barrow the path re-crosses the Fosse Way and soon enters the outstandingly beautiful village of Castle Combe. From here it starts to follow the richly wooded By Brook Valley and it keeps reasonably close to this stream until the latter flows into the Avon just beyond Bathford, but first going through the villages of Ford and Slaughterford, the one a hostage to the busy A420 and the other, enviably hidden away below wooded hillsides.

Leaving the course of the Macmillan Way the Cross-Cotswold just misses much of the village of Box, a village made famous, firstly by its great underground quarries, the source of much of Bath's stone, and secondly by the long railway tunnel through the hill above, built by the great railway engineer, Isambard K Brunel. It now heads westwards, still beside the By Brook, and crosses the Avon before joining the towpath of the Kennet and Avon Canal. It then follows this into Bath to reach this city's lovely Abbey - the end of its 86-mile course from Banbury.

Bath Abbey is also the southern terminus of the 100-mile long Cotswold Way and should you wish to complete the whole Cotswold Round, this is your opportunity! *For more about the Cotswold Round, turn to page 6.*

Bath Abbey - the end of our journey

How to Use this Guide

This guide to the 86-mile-long cross-Cotswold Pathway is in two parts: The first, an introductory section giving some of the background to its creation and use. The second, a detailed description of the path itself, divided into three chapters, varying in length according to the appropriate stopping and starting points. The Key Map inside the front cover shows the individual map coverage while the Contents is shown on the Title Page opposite including the map content of each chapter.

Each of the 19 double-page spreads is entirely self-contained, with map, text and possible illustration all inter-relating. This will ensure that when the book is opened out and inserted into a transparent map case, it can stay there until the next map section is reached. The maps are at a scale of 1:50,000 (about one-and-a-quarter inches to the mile) and are based upon the Ordnance Survey's Landranger series. The sheet numbers of the Ordnance Survey's Landranger, Outdoor Leisure, Explorer and Pathfinder maps covering the area similar to that covered by each of our own maps are also indicated. It should be noted that any remaining Pathfinder maps are soon to be replaced by Explorer maps.
The symbols and conventional signs used on the maps are explained in the block below.

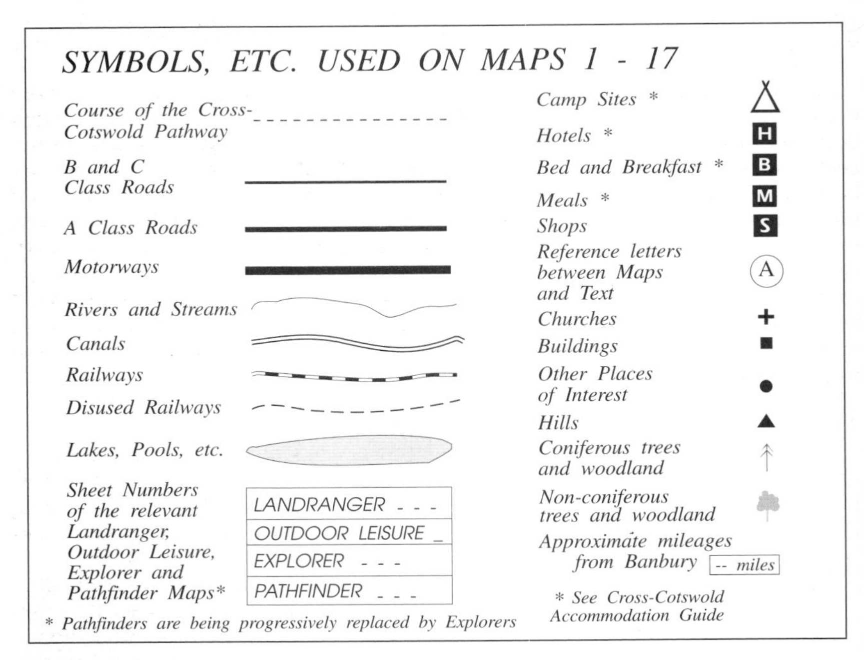

Each paragraph of text starts with a reference letter and this cross-refers with the same letter on the accompanying map. All information not concerned with the main Cross-Cotswold Pathway route is shown in italics, while the route details themselves are in normal type. It will also be noted that progressive mileages from Banbury are clearly displayed on every map and this will allow users to work out very simply the distance between any two points. It will also enable users to see how far they have gone and, by subtracting from the total of 86, to work out how far they are away from Bath. There is also a mileage chart on page 7 The 19 maps show the location of hotels, bed and breakfasts and meal places, either indicating their presence by being appended to the name of the appropriate town or village, or if well outside any town or village, their exact location. Details of these facilities are constantly changing and are not therefore included in this guide. However these details will be found in the small frequently updated supplementary leaflet, *The Cross-Cotswold Pathway Accommodation Guide*, which is available from the Macmillan Way Association, St Mary's Barn, Pillerton Priors, Warwick CV35 0PG. Please send a stamped and addressed envelope and a cheque *(made payable to the Macmillan Way Association)* for £1, all of which will be passed directly to Macmillan Cancer Relief (if you wish to send more it would be gratefully received!).

Castle Combe (see page 42)

With the help of information in this guidebook it should be possible to follow the Cross-Cotswold Pathway without further guidance. However, the route from Banbury to Bath is also waymarked with Macmillan Way waymarks, apart from sections using public roads and at one or two points where landowners have not been prepared to have our waymarks on their property. The waymarks are of two types - a self-contained plastic roundel with arrow and Macmillan Way logo, and a self-adhesive sticker with Macmillan Way logo, which is stuck on a standard yellow or blue waymark arrow (yellow for footpath and blue for bridleway). We hope that you have no difficulties, but if any are encountered it would be appreciated if you could let us have the details - *The Macmillan Way Association, St Mary's Barn, Pillerton Priors, Warwick CV35 0PG.* This will help us maintain the existing trail and improve it where necessary.

Walk Macmillan - Support Macmillan

The Cross-Cotswold Pathway and its big-brother, the Macmillan Way have been developed as a tribute to Douglas Macmillan, the founder of the organisation now known as Macmillan Cancer Relief and they are being used by an increasing number of people who have discovered the particular pleasure of walking across country. If you haven't tried it yet - now is the time!

We are also hoping that these pathways will help to raise funds for Macmillan Cancer Relief (see page 8) and with this in mind, might we suggest that you 'sponsor' yourselves for a small sum per mile and ask your friends and relations to help out by also becoming your sponsors. When you have finished your walk we could, should you so wish, let you have a Certificate of Congratulations. If you have managed to collect some sponsorship money (either from yourself, or from your friends and relations), this would of course be gratefully acknowledged on your Certificate.

* * * * * * *

Do let us have your comments , both on the Pathway itself, and on the way we are organising it. They would be very welcome. Letters to: *The Macmillan Way Association, St Mary's Barn, Pillerton Priors, Warwick CV35 0PG.*

Introducing the Cotswold Round

This 207-mile route has been devised by the Macmillan Way Association to provide walkers with a circular path around the best of the Cotswold Country. Being circular it can be started from any point, although Banbury and Bath are the best options for most people as they are so well placed on main rail and bus routes.

The Cotswold Round is made up of three separate elements - the **Cross-Cotswold Pathway** from Banbury to Bath, the very well established **Cotswold Way** from Bath to Chipping Campden and, completing the circle, the new **Cotswold Link** from Chipping Campden to Banbury. It should be noted that both the Cross Cotswold Pathway and the Cotswold Link are, at the moment, only described in a clockwise direction.

The 86-mile Cross-Cotswold Pathway, based largely on the Macmillan Way, is described in this guidebook. The 100-mile Cotswold Way is described in a South-to-North direction in *The Cotswold Way - The Complete Walker's Guide*, by Mark Richards and published by Penguin Books. The 28-mile Cotswold Link is described in a special leaflet produced by the Macmillan Way Association and is available from them at *St Mary's Barn, Pillerton Priors, Warwick CV35 0PG*. Please write for the latest price-list of our publications. These are listed on the rear cover of this guide, but are not priced.

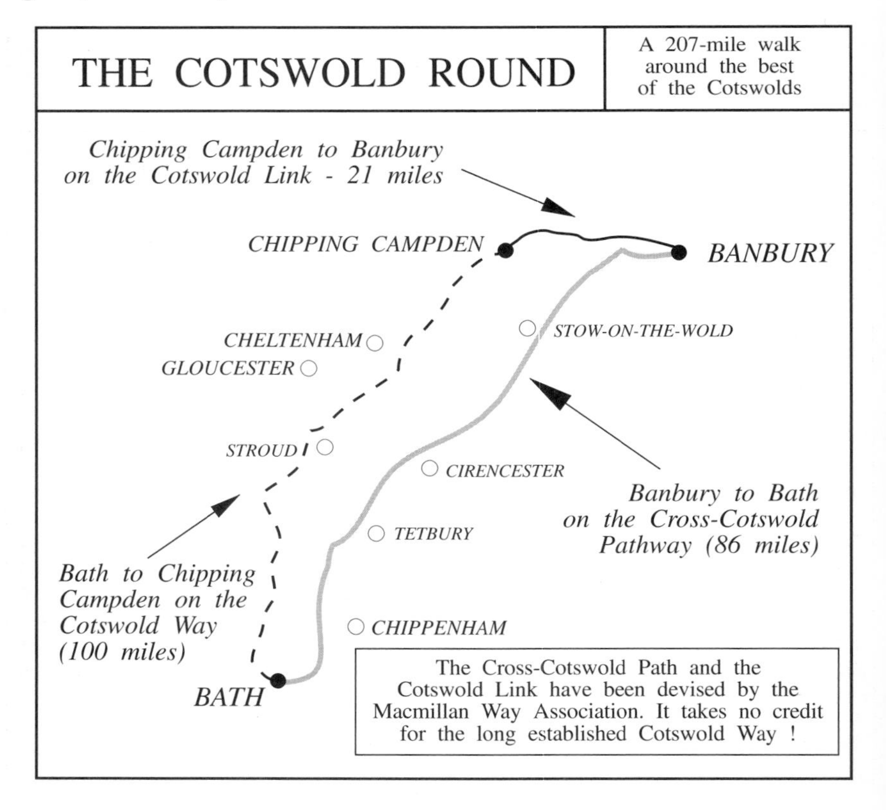

ORDNANCE SURVEY MAP COVERAGE OF THE CROSS-COTSWOLD PATHWAY

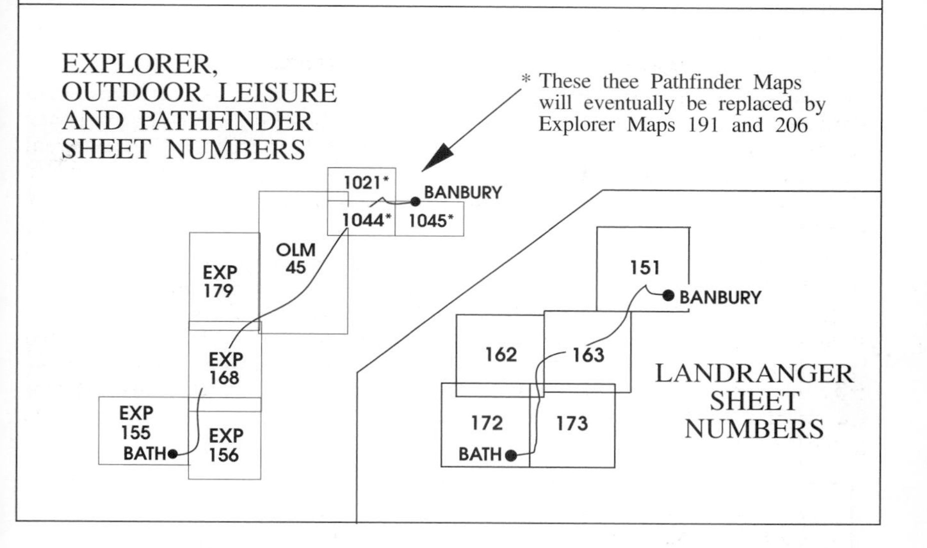

A LIST OF TOWNS AND VILLAGES ON THE CROSS-COTSWOLD PATHWAY WITH MILEAGES FROM BANBURY AND BATH

BANBURY	0	86
North Newington	2	84
Broughton	3	83
Swalcliffe	5	81
Epwell	7	79
Whichford	12	74
Long Compton	14	72
Chastleton	18	68
Adlestrop	19	67
Oddington	21	65
Maugersbury	23	63
Lower Slaughter	26	60
Cold Aston	28	58
Turkdean	30	56
Hampnett	32	54
Yanworth	34	52
Chedworth	36	50
Rendcomb	39	47
Woodmancote	41	45
Duntisbourne Rouse	43	43
Sapperton	46	40
Tunnel House Inn	48	38
Tarlton	49	37
Hazleton	52	34
Cherington	54	32
Avening	56	30
Chavenage	58	28
Westonbirt	62	24
Sherston	65	21
Luckington	67	19
Littleton Drew	70	16
Castle Combe	73	13
Ford	75	11
Slaughterford	76	10
Box	80	6
Bathford	83	3
Bathampton	84	2
BATH	86	0

Macmillan cancer relief

Macmillan Cancer Relief owes its existence to the vision of one man - Douglas Macmillan, who in 1911 looked on helplessly as his father suffered and eventually died of cancer. Moved by such needless pain and suffering the national charity was established with the aim of improving the public's and health professionals' knowledge of cancer and of understanding the needs of people with cancer and improving their lives. These aims remain as true now as they were then, with Macmillan Cancer Relief working towards the day when everyone will have equal and ready access to the best information, treatment and care for cancer.

Macmillan nurses work as part of a team, with other nurses and doctors, sharing their knowledge and skills

Macmillan Cancer Relief is probably best known for its specialist nurses. There are now over 1600 Macmillan nurses, specialists in cancer care, offering expert information and advice, skills in pain and symptom management and psychological and emotional support for people with cancer and their families. Macmillan nurses are employed by the NHS and they work as part of a team, sharing their knowledge and skills with other health professionals, helping to raise the standards of cancer care and ensuring that care for patients is continuous.

Macmillan also funds Macmillan doctors, buildings for cancer treatment and care and grants for patients in financial difficulties - services which help make the lives of people with cancer and their families easier, and reduce unnecessary levels of fear.

Macmillan nurses provide practical and emotional support to people with cancer and their families

We hope that the Macmillan Way and the Cross-Cotswold Pathway, with which it is associated, will help to increase public awareness of Macmillan and raise funds to help provide more services for people with cancer. One in three people in the UK will get cancer at some stage in their life, so directly or indirectly it affects us all. With your support Macmillan can help more people living with cancer.

Macmillan Cancer Relief Information Line: 0845 601 6161
www.macmillan.org.uk

The Country Code

Enjoy the countryside and respect its life and work - **Guard against all risk of fire** - **Fasten all gates** - **Keep your dogs under close control** - *keeping them on leads when there is any chance of encountering stock. Don't forget that pregnant ewes are very much at risk even from merely playful dogs* - **Keep to public paths across farmland** *and walk in single file to minimise path-spread or crop damage* - **Use gates and stiles to cross fences, hedges and walls** - **Leave livestock, crops and machinery alone** - **Take your litter home** - *nice thought, but if you are some days away from home, dump it in a litter bin in the next village you pass through. Don't forget that litter is not only untidy, but it can also cause great harm to animals and farm machinery* - **Help to keep all water clean** - **Make no unnecessary noise** - **Protect wildlife, plants and trees** - **Take special care on country roads**, *usually walk towards oncoming traffic, but on blind bends walk on the outside of the bend where you will be most visible (we have tried to minimise the use of dangerous roads, but there are a few stretches which require great care).*

A Friendly Countryside for All

While planning the Macmillan Way, the Cross-Cotswold Pathway and the Cotswold Link we have received great kindness from many land owners and tenant farmers and we have assured them that walkers along our path will go quietly through their land and that you will not give offence. If you look at things from country people's point of view, they are far more likely to appreciate yours.

When meeting anyone on your journey, take time to stop and pass the time of day with them. Many farmers and farm workers to whom we have talked, say how surprised they are by the number of walkers who just plod by without even saying hello. Stop to talk and you could well learn so much more about the country through which you are passing. Don't be discouraged if you don't always get a response, but keep trying - the overall result will be well worthwhile, and the next walkers that come along are more likely to have a friendly welcome. We have all got to live together, so please - let co-operation be your watchword, rather than confrontation, We are sure that you won't regret it.

Broughton Castle gatehouse and the nearby church

Chapter 1 Banbury - Maugersbury 23 Miles

Before setting out on your journey, try to spare time to look round Banbury. This has been a busy market town for many centuries and is now an important industrial centre. Despite much development it still has a few old alleys and quiet corners. Banbury Cross, our starting point is a 19th-century monument replacing a medieval cross destroyed by the Puritans in the early 17th-century. The interesting Museum and Information Centre, near the Cross, normally have the famous Banbury Cakes for sale and they also serve coffee and tea.

(A) Start by heading south-westwards from Banbury Cross, situated in the middle of a busy traffic-island. From here take the B4035 initially up West Bar Street (SP *Shipston-on-Stour*). Pass at least two inns on right - the Horse and Jockey and the Flowing Well. After about half-a-mile, turn right at large roundabout into Woodgreen Avenue - a wide double-track road with grass between tracks (SP - *Woodgreen Leisure Centre*). Now take first turn left, up Bretch Hill Road, then passing two traffic-calming chicanes. Bend to right and pass third chicane, and immediately pass semi-detached houses on left, the first of which is called 'The Spinney' and the second is Number 119.

(B) Immediately beyond Number 119 and before Number 121, turn left up into area with prefab garages on right. Go past garages and when in front of gates to covered reservoir, water tower and radio mast, turn sharp right to follow path through bushes. Bear left into field and go diagonally right, away from reservoir, aiming for gap in hedge and soon joining better defined path. Through gap in hedge and go in same direction across edge of next field keeping hedge to immediate right. At end of field turn right through gap in hedge and immediately bear left into next field and go down it with hedge to immediate left. Fine Oxfordshire Cotswolds views ahead and over to right. Follow hedge as it bends to left, through gap in hedge to left and immediately turn right to follow down with hedge now to right. Go straight over X-roads of paths (ignoring Banbury Fringe Walks sign) and into sparsely wooded area with small, denser wood to right. Now go down well-used path in scrubby woodland area, with fence on left for short distance. At end of woodland bear slightly right and then left to follow down field with hedge on immediate right. North Newington clearly visible ahead.

(C) Over two small concrete bridges crossing the Sor Brook by a sluice. Keep on path beyond bridges, passing small plantation on left and ignoring stile on left. Keep up left-hand side of field but shortly before

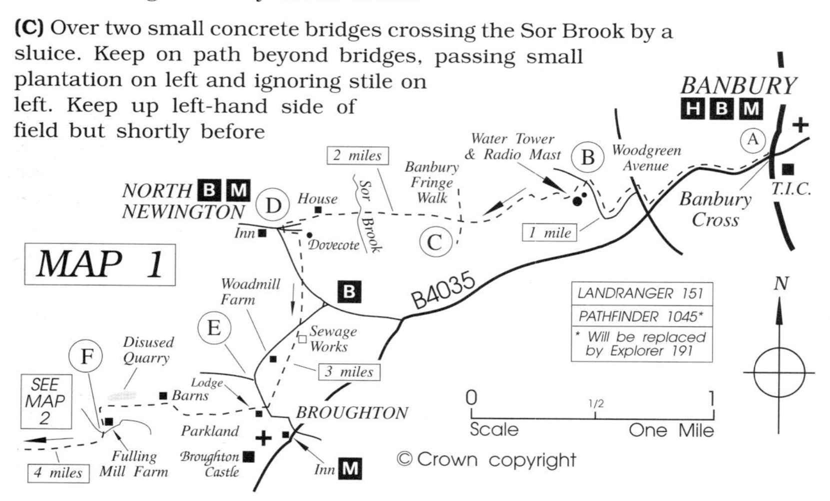

reaching house, turn left over stile and turn right to go up field, veering slightly away from wall and hedge on right. At top of field go over stile beside metal gate in wall. Cross minute paddock with barn conversion to left and bear left on to tarmac drive at entry to North Newington. Bear right on to public road into village and, immediately beyond house on left called *Homeward*, turn left up short surfaced path. Turn left onto public road with *Yew Tree House* facing. *(But turn right if you wish to visit the Blinking Owl Inn, which is on left just beyond nearby road junction.)*

Broughton Castle

(D) Immediately beyond Grafton Cottage on right, turn right up narrow pathway with house and stone wall to right and wooden fencing to left. Over stile and go across semi-parkland aiming straight ahead towards gateway at top, right-hand end of drive. Attractive circular dovecote down to left. Go down into valley and up again to go through large gateway over cattlegrid and turn left with care onto public road. Almost immediately turn right over stile to cross field on grassy headland between two cropped areas. Through large gap and go diagonally right, across road with care. Over stile to head diagonally right, down across field aiming for spire of Broughton Church. Over stile in bottom left-hand corner of field, across concrete roadway with sewage works gate to immediate left and through gap in hedge crossing small bridge. *(If for any reason this next field is impassable, go up concrete roadway and turn left to walk down road as far as lodge - see below.)* Keep in same direction across large field still aiming for church spire. Eventually veer slightly right and go through large wooden gate in front of small lodge. *(But turn left and go up road if you wish to visit the Saye and Sele Arms.)*

(E) Cross road with care and go slightly right before going left over stone stile into Broughton Castle's park, now veering slightly to right of garden fence-line. Walk almost due west across fine parkland with views of church and beautifully moated Broughton Castle down to left. *Built in 1306, Broughton Castle is the home of Lord Saye and Sele. A handsome front was added in Elizabethan times and many interior improvements carried out, but this has not disturbed Broughton's exceptionally romantic atmosphere. The adjoining church is also well worth visiting.*

Once over brow, aim to right of right-hand woodlands on far side of park and at end of park go over stile. Now go down field towards barns with fence on immediate left. Just before barns, turn left through metal gate and immediately over stile. Now bear right and follow right-hand edge of field with fence and hedge on immediate right. Over stile beside large wooden gate and keep along top of field with fence on immediate right, with large, long-disused quarry beyond. Fulling Mill Farm now down to left. Through large metal gate and turn left down partly surfaced farm track.

(F) Pass Fulling Mill Farm on our left and over old mill leat with stream just beyond. Immediately through gate and bear right up track with small beech wood on left. Good view back to Fulling Mill Farm. Through metal gate and continue up track, with large open field to right and hedge to left. *Now on the course of a Roman road that ran from Alcester and Stratford towards Kings Sutton, south of Banbury. We shall be following it until we reach Epwell, although it is never very apparent.* Pass small barn on left and soon over slight brow before dropping down quite steeply to public road.

(A) Over public road with care and continue in same direction on an even smaller public road (Restriction Sign - *3-T*). Tadmarton Church visible over to left. Soon turn right at Y-junction keeping on wider road *(But bear left if you wish to visit the Lampet Arms, Tadmarton - half a mile).* Rounded hill ahead is Madmarston Hill, which was once topped by a fortified earthwork of uncertain age. Swalcliffe Church visible ahead left. Pass entrance gates to Swalcliffe Lea on left and soon cross course of footpath running from Shutford and Tadmarton. *In the 1960's a Romano-British settlement was excavated in field to right, just below Madmarston Hill, but there is now no trace of this above ground.* Straight, not left, leaving public road and going on to bridleway (SP - *Bridleway*) *(But turn left if you wish to visit the Stag's Head Inn, Swalcliffe - three quarters of a mile).* Straight, not left, at junction of tracks (SP - *Epwell*) and go through small gate beside large metal gate.

Course of the Roman road near Madmarston Hill

(B) At top of rise go through small metal gate beside large metal gate and over public road with care. Keep in same direction going through opposite gate (SP - *Epwell*) and keep to edge of field with hedge on immediate right - track now unsurfaced, but still on course of Roman road. Through small metal gate in valley crossing small stream and keep in same direction with hedge to immediate right. Farmington Farm just visible over to right and Blenheim Farm visible ahead, below to left. Veer to right to go through hedge and continue in same direction with hedge now to left and fence on right for short distance only. Path soon becomes track again, going between two hedges and soon dropping down into valley. Attractive fishing lake visible over to left. Pass entrance on left to lake area (private) and large tank just beyond. Go straight over X-roads of tracks, through large double gates (with ruins of Woodington Barn up to right) and

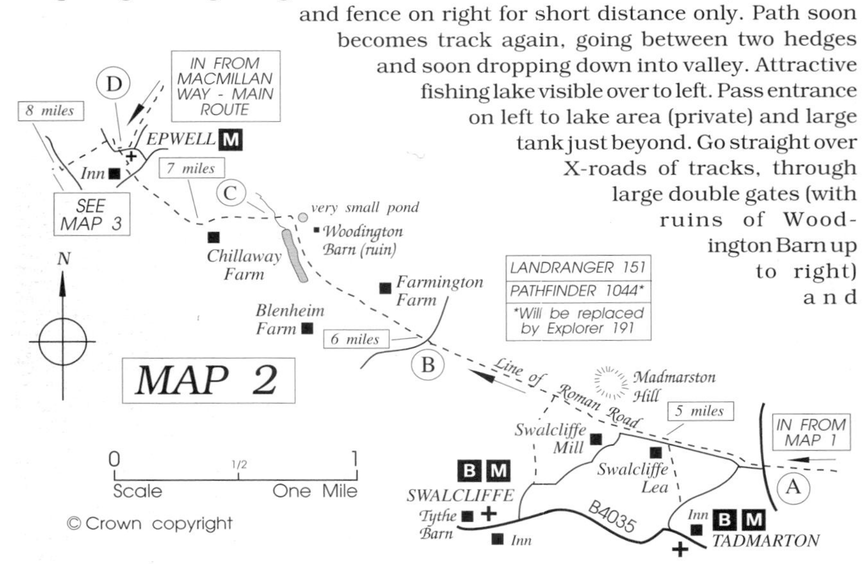

Epwell Church

into field, keeping hedge (with stream beyond) to left and aiming for left-hand corner.

(C) Go between hedge to left and small pond to right (possibly dry in summer) and turn left to go through metal gate below power pole. Over sleeper bridge crossing small stream and **keep in same direction as bridge**, going up field with young plantation and then hedge to immediate left (if field is pasture cut across indent by plantation and then join hedge beyond). Chillaway Farm visible ahead left. Near top of field go onto track between hedge to left and another young plantation to right. Soon through large metal gate and keep up paddock in same direction with hedge now on immediate right and Chillaway Farm well over to left. At top of paddock turn right through large metal gate and go along bottom of next field keeping hedge on immediate right. Good views of Yarn Hill and Epwell Hill across valley to right. Start to drop down slightly as Epwell comes into view ahead. Through small wooden gate and keep down field in same direction first going below two trees, then pass pond on left and garden over hedge to right. Bend round slightly to right by first house in Epwell and through large wooden gate into village. Immediately bear left at intersection of tracks on sloping green, noting old well head down to right. Almost immediately cross public road and go up narrow pathway with cottage on left and wall on right (no sign). *But go up road if you wish to visit The Chandler's Arms, which is just beyond the cottage.* Note old semi-circular bread-oven projecting into pathway beside cottage. At top of this short path, turn right and follow grassy sward bearing left around outer edge of field. Now pass village playground on left and churchyard just beyond on right. *Sitting low down in an attractive churchyard, Epwell church has a small central tower, a thin Jacobean pulpit and a pretty little 14th-century piscina.*

(D) At end of churchyard, turn left on to public road *(joining the main Macmillan Way, which has come down from Boston on the Lincolnshire coast)* and then, keeping on road, bear round to right. Almost immediately turn left just beyond 30 MPH de-restriction signs and up steps onto pathway between private gardens. Bear slightly right in field and head up to left of hedge-line on right. Over stile at end of field and turn right and then left to follow right-hand edge of field aiming for radio mast on horizon. (Ignore waymarks on stile to right.) Through metal gate and keep in same direction.

Our path beyond Epwell

(A) Through large wooden gate, turn right onto road and very soon turn left through metal gate. Head straight across field aiming to right of radio mast and over stile about 50 yards to right of mast. Turn left onto Ditchedge Lane, *a green road that here forms the boundary between Oxfordshire and Warwickshire. This trackway may have been part of a prehistoric trade route, but it is more likely to have Anglo-Saxon origins. Although there is now no ditch alongside it, there may once have been one marking the boundary between the two counties.* We shall now follow Ditchedge Lane for some two-and-a-half miles and route-finding will be comparatively simple. Much of the lane is on a ridge and there are fine views both to right and left. Pass radio mast on left and into more sheltered length of lane, with pleasant glimpses to right of the spire of Winderton church, the impressive tower of Brailes church and Brailes Hill, topped with its clump of trees.

(B) Go straight ahead joining B4035 for short distance, before bearing left at next bend just beyond Warwickshire County sign, re-joining Ditchedge Lane. Keep straight along this green road with its fine views both to left and right. At end of third field on left, pass unsigned bridleway to left running between parallel hedges and leading to Sibford Gower - a possible diversion. *It would be possible to re-join main route further along Ditchedge Lane, or beyond Traitor's Ford.* Just beyond Round Hill to right, at end of hedge-bordered section of Ditchedge Lane, through gate into field following same line as lane and still following county boundary, with hedge to immediate left. Now start to drop down into upper valley of River Stour with fine views over to right including Broadway Tower, on the distant Cotswold skyline almost due west. At bottom of long field follow path along small sunken section of track and through gate onto minor road.

(C) Bear left and over bridge beside attractive ford with woodland on both sides of road. *This is known as Traitor's Ford, but the origins of its name are shrouded in mystery - some think that a traitor was killed here, others believe that its was once known as Traders' Ford, the traders using it during their journeys with pack animals along Ditchedge Lane.* Up wooded hill on minor road, soon going straight, not left, at first road junction (SP - *Whichford*) and then turning right at second road junction (SP - *Whichford*). Keep on minor road for about half-a-mile.

(D) At first hedge-line on left beyond New Barn farm buildings turn left through gateway. Go up track keeping to immediate left of fence and hedge-line. Bear right through first gate and then over stile. Go half right, follow slight signs of track down field and over stile beside gate at bottom of field. Down hill keeping to left of scanty hedge and tree line and at its end, bear half-left heading for bottom left-hand corner of field. Over stile and bridge, up small lane into quiet valley hamlet of Ascott and soon turn right onto path immediately beyond gates of first house on right. Up narrow path between hedge and fence and over small stile into old orchard. Over second stile and turn left onto minor cul-de-sac road.

In Whichford Wood, just beyond Point G

(E) Turn right at x-rds by Coombe House and follow path beside minor road heading towards Whichford. Bear left at road junction by small triangular green and enter Whichford, *an unspoilt village below the steep scarp face of the Oxfordshire Cotswolds.* Keep straight, not left, at wide village green (SP - *Stourton*) and pass Norman Knight Inn on right.

Bear left by War Memorial at end of green with telephone box on left. Pass elegant 18th-century Old Rectory on right and church just beyond on right. *Whichford church has a Norman south doorway, an early 14th-century tower and a beautiful Perpendicular clerestory.*

(F) Well beyond church turn left up Roman Row - a small housing estate. Remains of medieval moat visible over to right at this junction. Over stile on left at end of Roman Row. Continue in same direction with hedge on right and at end of hedge turn half-right to go diagonally up hill following imprecise track towards oak and ash tree. Beyond these trees, keep just outside left-hand edge of Whichford Wood for about a mile, passing through gaps in two cross--hedges before reaching an X-roads of tracks. **(Now keep alert - some walkers have gone wrong here!)** Keep straight ahead on track now going between a tall hedge to its left and wood still to its right. But after about 100 yards veer right as track fully enters wood and drops down into valley.

(G) After nearly a quarter-of-a-mile turn left just beyond valley bottom onto track leading down valley. Through gateway at end of woods into field, keeping on track along right-hand edge of field with hedge and fence to immediate right. Long Compton church visible in valley ahead. Through metal gate beyond woods on right, still keeping on track, with hedge now to immediate left and open field up to right. Through gate at end of field and continue on harder surfaced track, which is now between two high hedges. Through metal gate and head straight across field passing large pond on left (Signed - *'Danger'*) and through metal gate to left of house. Onto surfaced driveway at entry to Long Compton and turn left with care onto A3400 (SP - *Woodstock*).

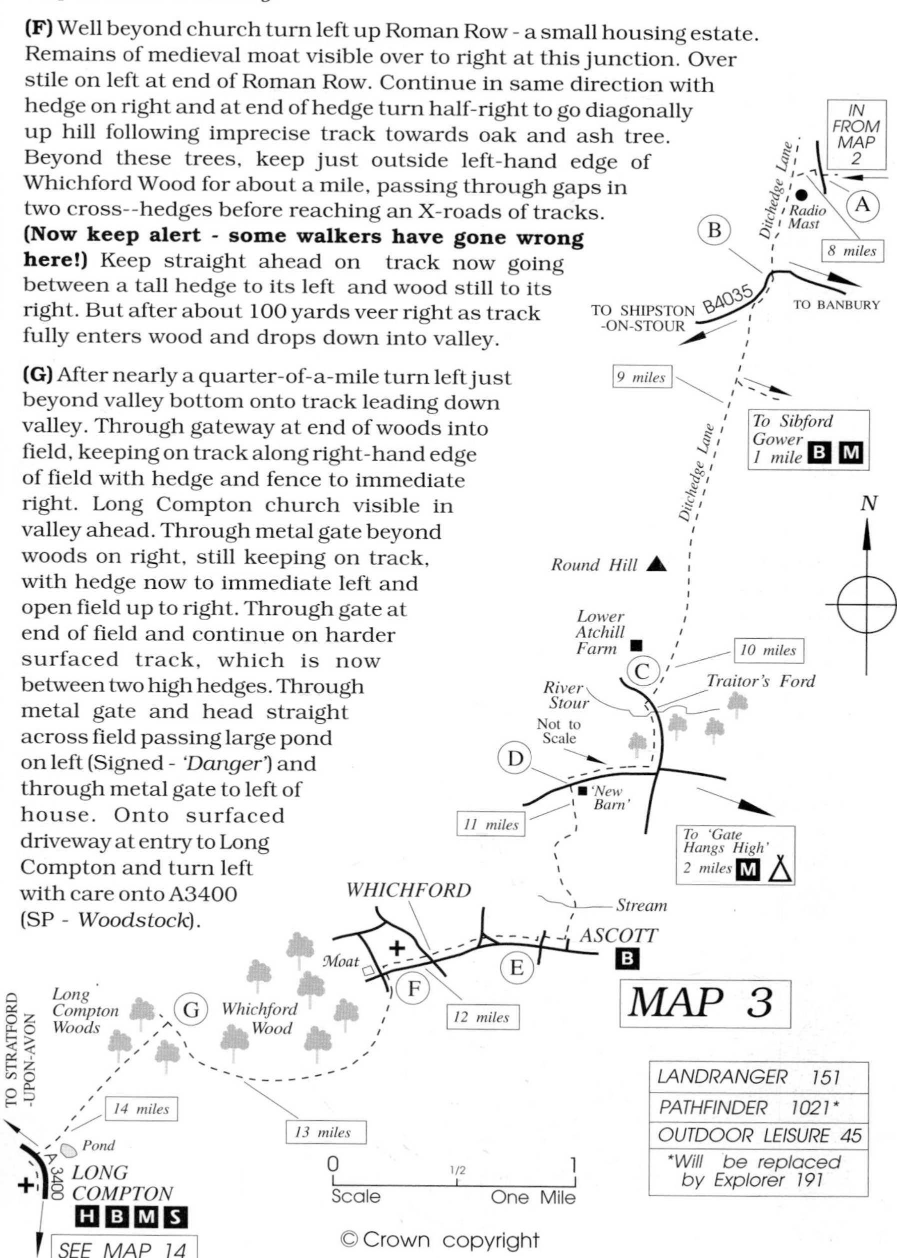

(A) Having turned left onto A3400, follow it through Long Compton, keeping to pathway on left. *Sitting beneath the high Cotswold edge, Long Compton has many attractive stone houses and cottages strung out along the still busy A3400.* Pass Crockwell Street on right *(go down here and soon onto path if you wish to use camp site at Mill Farm - three-quarters-of-a-mile). Pass church on right with its handsome Perpendicular tower and charming thatched lych-gate.* Manor House (B&B) on left, Post Office Stores on right. Base of old cross on stone plinth on right just beyond. Pass road to left signed B&B, which leads to telephone box and to Butler's Road Farm.

(B) Just beyond this road junction, turn right off A3400 beyond Village Hall on right, going through wooden gate with stone gate pier to left inscribed 'Daddy's Bank'. *(But go straight ahead for few yards if you wish to visit Red Lion Hotel and Restaurant.)* Through second wooden gate and head slightly left across field, first going on part of concrete track, to go through gate in wooden fence. Keep in same direction to go over stile beside metal gate, then go slightly left and bear right to follow well surfaced private road with hedge to right *(it may be possible to follow path to right of hedge - if so, this will be clearly marked)*. Leave surfaced track where it bends to right and continue in same direction on rougher track keeping hedge and ditch on immediate right and passing large converted barn beyond hedge on right. Where track bends to right, go straight ahead up field and then bear slightly left to head for far left-hand, top corner.

(C) Over stile at this corner and head straight up hill across field following well used path, keeping to immediate right of spring. South Hill Farm soon visible ahead. Through metal gate and first head towards centre of farm buildings, but soon converging with hedge line on right. Bear right over stile and follow line of hedge on right, with farm buildings to left. Where hedge finishes, keep in same direction across field, aiming well to right of radio mast with reflectors.

(D) Over stone stile and join road keeping in same direction and return briefly into Oxfordshire. *(But if you wish to visit the Bronze Age stone circle known as the Rollright Stones, turn left onto road, go straight, not left, turn left and go straight not left again - about one mile. This diversion is worthwhile and not as difficult to reach as the route directions would imply!)* Back on main route again - fine views westwards to Gloucestershire Cotswolds over to right. Just beyond point where road bends to right, go through metal gate on left (back into Warwickshire) and immediately bear right onto bridleway to follow along left-hand side of wall, thus continuing in same general direction. Oakham Farm soon visible down to right and good views ahead right, out over Evenlode Valley. Soon, near point where wall comes in from right, cross to right-hand side of our parallel wall, but continue in same direction. Follow farm track in same direction for about a mile with Little Compton visible down to right. *(Watch for left turn onto bridleway if you wish to visit Cross Hands Inn - meals and camping.)*

Chastleton House

Through small metal gate beside large one below power-pole with transformer, and note sign beyond on left regarding quarry workings. Keep in same direction with quarry to left and wall to right.

(E) Pass quarry and farm buildings on left, **cross busy A44 with great care** and onto minor road. Entrance to Grey Goose Farm on left of main route just beyond A44. Through gate beside cattle-grid onto unfenced road, having just re-entered Oxfordshire and through pleasant parkland with grass and trees (Notice states - *Private Property - No Parking, Camping or Picnicking*). Pass two farmhouses down to right and at end of unfenced road through gate ignoring bridleway sign to left, and turn right onto minor road.

(F) Go down hill and soon, by kind permission of the National Trust, turn left into their car park. Go past small hut and down path across pleasant field and close to attractive 18th-century arched dovecote *(This is not a right-of-way. Please leave all gates as you find them)*. Turn left onto road and pass Chastleton House on right. *Extensively restored by the National Trust, this fine Stuart manor house was probably designed by Robert Smythson, the architect best known for Hardwick Hall in Derbyshire. It has a handsome five-gabled south front and an interior largely undisturbed by 18th- or 19th-century alteration, the most impressive feature of which is its Long Gallery at the top of the house.* Almost immediately turn left through large wooden gate *(not signed, as use of this next short section is kindly allowed for Macmillan Way walkers only, by the National Trust and the owner of nearby Harcombe, and is not a right-of-way)*. Through second wooden gate, up lovely avenue of trees and soon go through small metal gate passing from Oxfordshire into Gloucestershire and returning to right-of-way.

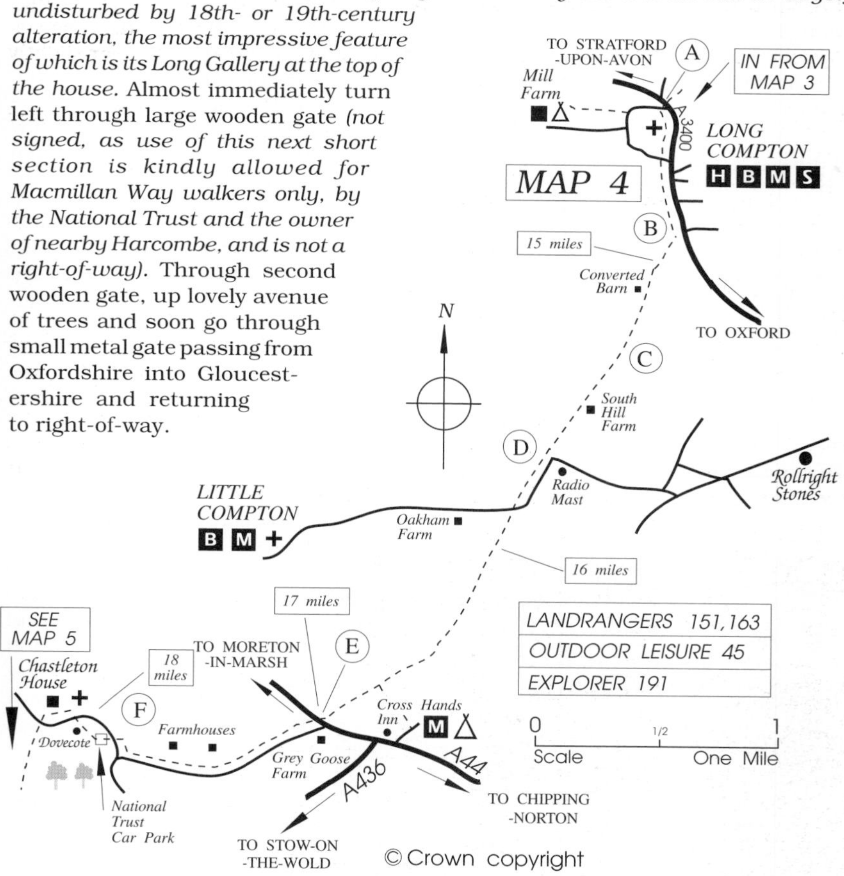

(A) Now head diagonally right, across field on well used track. Stow-on-the-Wold church just visible on skyline over to right. Over brow and start to drop down heading for waymark to left of two trees. Over stile by wooden gate beyond waymark and continue in same direction down field. Over stile following right-hand of two waymarks and continue down field keeping fairly close to right of hedge-line. Beyond large tree near end of field, bear left over stile, and immediately bear right, now keeping to left of remaining hedge-line and keeping in same direction. Soon over another stile with hedge converging from left. Initially follow line of hedge to immediate right, but where it bends to right, head diagonally left across field aiming for waymark on stile. Over this stile and onto track with hedge to left.

(B) Pass farm buildings on right and at entry to Adlestrop go over road junction onto minor road by bus shelter with the old Adlestrop Railway Station sign board. *This stands as a tribute to Edward Thomas, whose highly evocative poem* Adlestrop, *begins thus, 'Yes, I remember Adlestrop ...'. Sadly he died in France in 1917, aged only 39. His poem is recorded on a plaque on the seat.* Follow minor road into pretty Adlestrop village with its flower-filled cottage gardens and bear right by small Post Office (SP - Church). Bear right by church and then bear left down track between churchyard wall and Old Rectory; *this was often visited by Jane Austen, when her uncle, Theophilus Leigh, lived here.* Through small gate keeping on track between fences, with small lakes possibly just visible ahead and over to right. *Views back to Adlestrop Park, the south-west front of which was designed by gentleman-architect, Sanderson Miller of Radway in Warwickshire.* Through small gate beside large one and head diagonally right, and to immediate left of cricket pitch's low boundary fence. Skirt round about a third of cricket pitch's perimeter and then aim well to left of trees bordering possibly visible lake. After short distance head for footpath fingerpost now visible ahead.

(C) Over two stiles and turn left onto minor road. Almost immediately turn right with care onto A436 and keep on path along its right-hand side. *Over bridge crossing Isambard K. Brunel's London to Worcester railway line, with view to right of remains of station immortalised by Edward Thomas (see above).* Then over infant River Evenlode and soon cross to path on left-hand side of road. Turn left onto minor road (SP - *Lower Oddington*) and soon enter attractive village of Lower Oddington. Follow round long bend to right by Fox Inn and turn left at road junction by Post Office (SP - *St Nicholas Church*).

(D) At bottom of hill, turn right just before drive to New Rectory Farm on right, and over stile by gateway where road bends to left in valley. *But go straight ahead for 250 yards if you wish to visit fascinating St Nicholas's Church. This is an ambitious, largely 13th- and 14th-century building with a remarkably unspoilt interior. See especially the lovely old chancel roof and the extensive 'Doom' wall paintings.* Back on main route - go straight across middle of narrow field, through kissing-gate and continue in same direction keeping to immediate right of hedge. Through another kissing-gate, cross small brook and up narrow pathway between

Memories of Edward Thomas at Adlestrop

two walls with house on right. Join road at eastern end of Upper Oddington and continue in same direction passing drive on left to Latimer Farm. Bear left at road junction just beyond and up road for about a quarter-of-a-mile, with Horse and Groom Inn on right and telephone box on left.

(E) Keep on road out of Upper Oddington and turn right over stile just beyond last house on right. Down grass walk between two fences, over stile and head diagonally left aiming for yellow waymark just below power-pole in hedge across field. Do not go over waymarked stile but turn left to follow up to left of hedge. Where hedge turns to right, continue up across field aiming just to left of grass-covered reservoir. *Good views back from here include distant Brailes Hill, with its clump of trees and, much closer, Warren Hastings' beloved Daylesford House, built by him after retiring from his controversial career as Governor of Bengal.* Turn right through kissing gate to left of reservoir and go between reservoir fence on right and hedge on left. Into field keeping to immediate right of hedge and follow this line behind rugby club's pavilion and along left-hand edge of club's grounds for short distance only. Soon turn left through wooden gate and go along grassy track.

(F) Turn right onto B4450 and walk carefully along here on right-hand side to face oncoming traffic - road is quite busy and verges are narrow. Soon pass Fairview Farmhouse (B&B) on right and good view of Stow-on-the-Wold church ahead. Turn left off B4450 immediately before reaching the A436 (SP - *Maugersbury Village only*). Follow road into Maugersbury, *a pleasant village with lovely views across valley to Icomb Hill.*

(G) Bear left in Maugersbury by small green and telephone box on right (SP - *Maugersbury only*). *(But turn right if you wish to visit Stow-on-the-Wold - half-a-mile. To re-join main route at Map 17, Point A, walk down path beside A429 Fosse Way.) The attractive little market town of Stow-on-the-Wold is the focal point of the northern Cotswolds. Its Market Square is lively with visitors and local country shoppers all year long and it has all the facilities required by users of our Way including an excellent Tourist Information Centre and a number of B&Bs, hotels, inns and eating places.* Main route bears round to right keeping Dower House on left. Pass Manor Farm on right and keep out of village on road despite twin *No Through Road* signs.

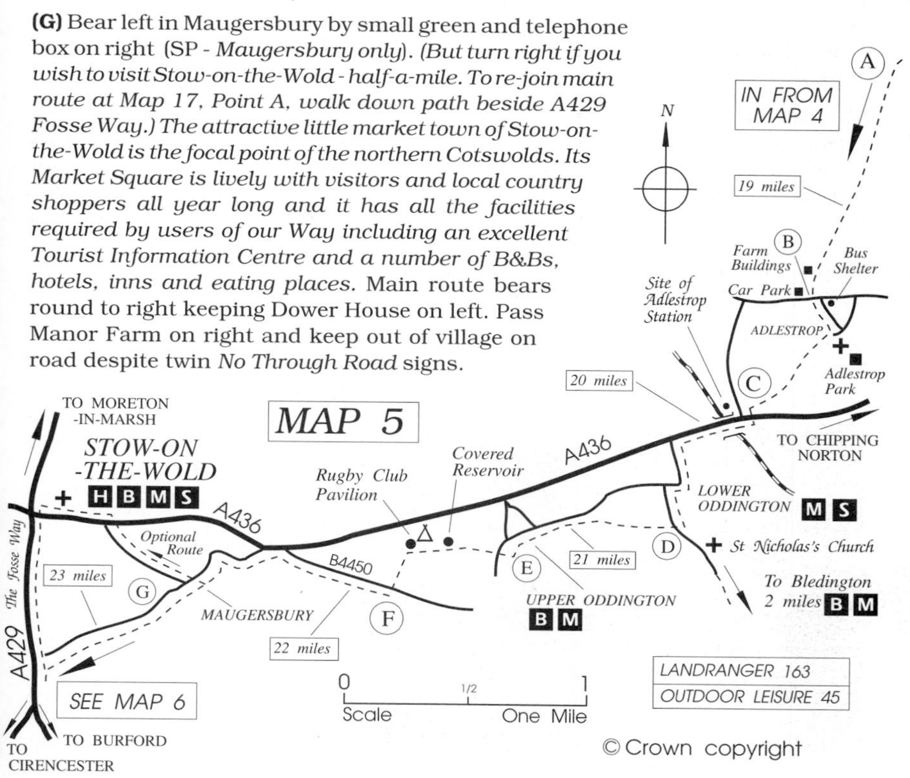

Chapter 2 Maugersbury (Stow-on-the-Wold) - The Tunnel House Inn, Coates 26 miles

(A) About a mile beyond Maugersbury, through road barrier and turn left to follow wide path down beside the very busy A429 (SP - *Cirencester*). (If you have taken the diversion via Stow-on-the-Wold, re-join the main route here.) *The A429 follows the course of the Fosse Way. This was built by the Romans a few years after their invasion of Britain in 43AD and ran for 182 miles, between Lincoln and Exeter. For much of its course the Cross-Cotswold Pathway runs parallel with the Fosse Way and it crosses it twice - here below Stow, and later, near Castle Combe in Wiltshire.* At bottom of hill turn right and **cross A429 by traffic lights with great care**. Go down left-hand of two drives (SP's - *Private Drive to Hyde Mill* and *Bridleway to Lower Swell*). Follow well surfaced road past woodlands, cottage and farm to arrive at gate into Hyde Mill driveway. Go through gate and between avenue of poplars before bearing right by Hyde Mill House.

(B) Turn left over bridge (SP - *Lower Slaughter*) crossing mill pound *(this is formed by the Dikler, a stream which rises at Donnington Brewery lake and which, at Bourton-on-the-Water, flows into the River Eye, itself a tributary of the better known Windrush. We shall now share paths with The Heart of England Way as far as Lower Slaughter. This 120-mile long-distance path runs between Milford in Staffordshire and Bourton-on-the-Water, just to the south of Lower Slaughter.* (Follow Heart of England waymarks as far as Lower Slaughter.) Keep straight past houses, then bear left (SP - *Lower Slaughter*). Bear right at end of last house (SP - *Lower Slaughter*) and along track. Over very small stream, turn left through gate and straight across field (very boggy here in winter), with little River Dikler on left. Over stile with Dikler just to left and head across field towards next gate with the Dikler veering away to left. Through gate and continue in same direction to cross fenced ditch before changing direction slightly to right. Cross another fenced ditch and almost immediately through gateway.

(C) Now head diagonally aiming for waymark by gateway near end of left-hand edge of field. Through gateway (SP - *Lower Slaughter*) and head for stile and gate at bottom right-hand corner of field. Through stile to right of gate and head diagonally across short field aiming for waymark. Over small bridge and stile and turn right to follow round edge of field before shortly turning left in corner, with wood now to right. Now aim straight towards Lower Slaughter Manor (now a hotel) along a broad grassy headland with hedge to immediate right. But just before end of field, turn right through metal gate and then immediately left, with hedge now on left, thus maintaining previous line. Over stile and into sports field keeping to its left-hand edge.

Lower Slaughter

(D) Through small wooden gate behind sports pavilion onto path at entry to Lower Slaughter. Now bear right onto driveway and then bear left onto road by corner of churchyard. Pass church on left and bear right at road junction by Washbourne Court Hotel (SP - *Upper Slaughter*). *Now briefly on the Wardens' Way - a 14-mile walking route between Bourton-on-the-Water and Winchcombe.* Walk up village on quieter, right-hand side of stream - the little River Eye, which flows into the River Windrush just below Bourton-on-the-Water. *Most of this delightful and much visited village seems almost to have been planted upon the banks of its stream. Stop here awhile if you are fortunate enough to arrive here at a quiet time.* Cross stream by small stone bridge (but go straight ahead if you wish to visit the interesting Old Mill Museum and Shop). Over 'main road' onto smaller road by Kingswell Cottage *(Now leaving the Wardens' Way)*. Leave Lower Slaughter and climb out of valley, but do look back at mill with its water wheel and little brick chimney.

(E) At T-junction cross minor road with care and onto track. Pass small wood in field to left as track levels out. Views of bustling Bourton-on-the-Water well over to left. Start gentle descent into Windrush Valley and cross road to go through small gate. *The road we have just crossed is known as Buckle Street. It acquired its name in Anglo-Saxon times, but its origins are probably much earlier.* Head diagonally right across large field aiming for far right-hand corner and go through small metal gate.

(F) Bear left onto well defined track with wall to left and soon through large metal gate. Keep on track with wall to immediate left (still dropping down into valley) and then through metal gate and down track, now overhung with trees, with narrow field to right. Bear right at junction of bridleways, *joining the Windrush Way - a 14-mile walking route between Winchcombe and Bourton-on-the-Water.* Down wide, surfaced path curving left to surfaced road with houses on right. Over River Windrush and immediately start to climb out of valley. Bear slightly left by entrance roadway to Aston Farm on right, *now leaving the Windrush Way. Few signs are now visible of railway line that once crossed road here.* Almost immediately bear right keeping on surfaced road, ignoring waymark on left. Up steep little pitch and then turn right off road to walk up field to immediate right of hedge and wall, which soon bears left by tree. Pleasant views back over the Windrush Valley from here.

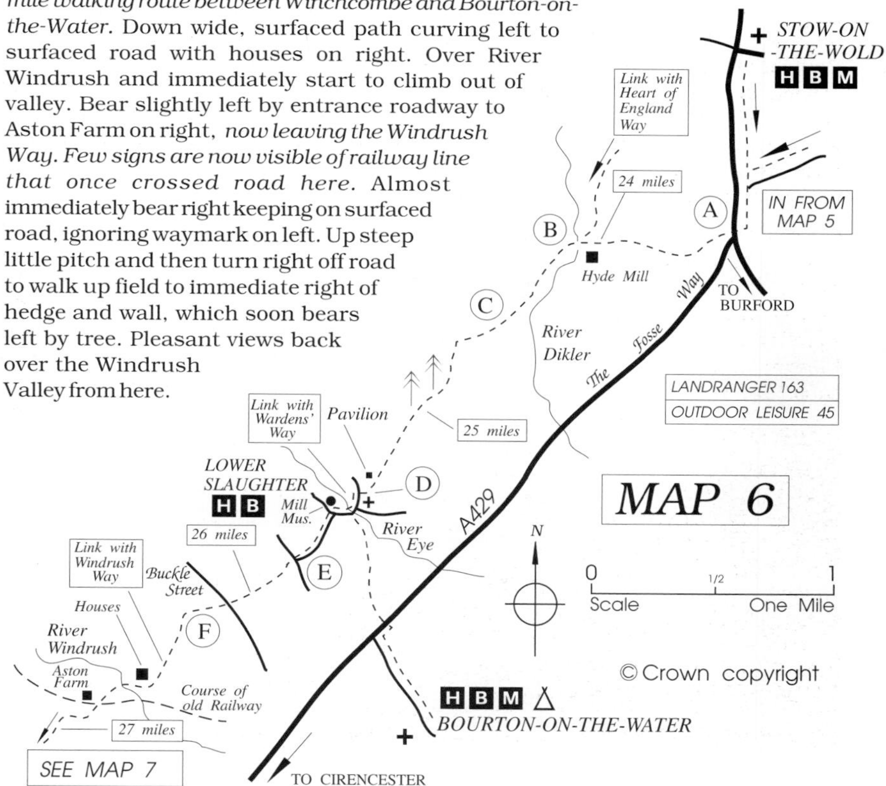

(A) Cross the busy A436 with great care, through double metal gates and keep to left-hand edge of field with wall on immediate left. *Now traversing some classic 'Cotswold country', with rolling wolds and wide open views; and if its early summer, skylarks will almost certainly be singing above.* Pass attractive clump of trees over to left which are sited on top of a Stone Age long barrow or burial mound. Follow hedge-line as it curves down to right and then bear left through gap in wall, passing to left of old farm vehicles, to farm track with buildings of Camp Farm down to right. Turn left onto track and almost immediately turn right to follow up left-hand side of field with hedge to left. Through gap in hedge converging from right, still keeping to left-hand edge of field.

(B) Bear right onto minor road just beyond small wood on left. (We shall now follow road into Cold Aston, with its church soon visible over to right.) Down hill into valley with woods soon on both sides and up road, noting alternative name for this village on its entry sign - Aston Blank. *Having visited this high wold village in winter, we feel that its usual name 'Cold Aston' is totally justifiable!* Bear half-left at Cold Aston's village green with its massive sycamore tree, telephone box and delightful inn, the Plough; taking small road to immediate left of inn. *But go straight ahead if you wish to visit the interesting, largely Norman church, with pleasant stone vaulting beneath its tower.* Keep straight past cottage called *Alberts* on right and over low stone stile at end of small road. Down narrow path with fence to left and wall to right, over second stile and turn right keeping fence on immediate right. Over third stile and through gate to pass in front of house with small ha-ha bordered lawn on right.

(C) Over fourth stile and bear left onto Bangup Lane, a surfaced track happily signed *Unfit for Motor Vehicles*, which we shall follow as far as Turkdean. Soon pass two houses on right, one known as Bangup Barn. After one-and-a-half miles go up attractive sunken road overhung with trees at entry to Turkdean.

(D) Turn left onto road by small triangular green in Turkdean and go through village. Pass *Old Shop* on left, with telephone box just beyond. *On left pass church in large churchyard bordered by chestnut trees. The interior has several interesting features including a Norman chancel arch and a medieval stone pulpit.* Turn right where road bends to left beyond horse trough on right, onto sunken footpath overhung with trees which leads down hill. Soon enter hamlet of Lower Dean on track with house on left. Over small bridge crossing stream, pass post box on right and bear right onto road by house over to left . Up hill on road leaving Lower Dean, soon passing Castle Barn Farm on left and woods on right.

Bangup Lane, well beyond Cold Aston

(E) Straight, not right at minor road junction

(SP - *Hampnett*) and immediately **cross busy A40 with great care**, to join minor road (SP - *Hampnett village only*). Pass Hampnett entry sign and start to drop down into this minute village, its wide green having houses thinly spread around it. Through gate and keep on road through village, soon passing trough on left of road which is source of River Leach. *This flows south-eastwards from here to join the Thames just below Lechlade. The nearby, largely Norman church has an unusual interior decorated in 'medieval style' in the 1880s.* Turn right onto small road leading down hill by telephone box with church just beyond on left (SP - *No Through Road*). *(But go straight ahead, past church and then bear half-right onto path down valley if you wish to visit Northleach, with its Countryside Museum, Mechanical Music Museum and fine wool church - one mile).*

(F) Back on main route (having turned right) - bear left keeping on surfaced road where infant River Leach flows beneath it and almost immediately turn right onto path just before road becomes private drive. Up path with walls on both sides and through wooden gate into field. Route is now straight ahead to corner of wall ahead, then along fence/hedge on right-hand edge of field and down slope to go through small gate. Straight across field in deep valley aiming for stile just to left of junction of wall lines. Over stile and keep to immediate left of wall.

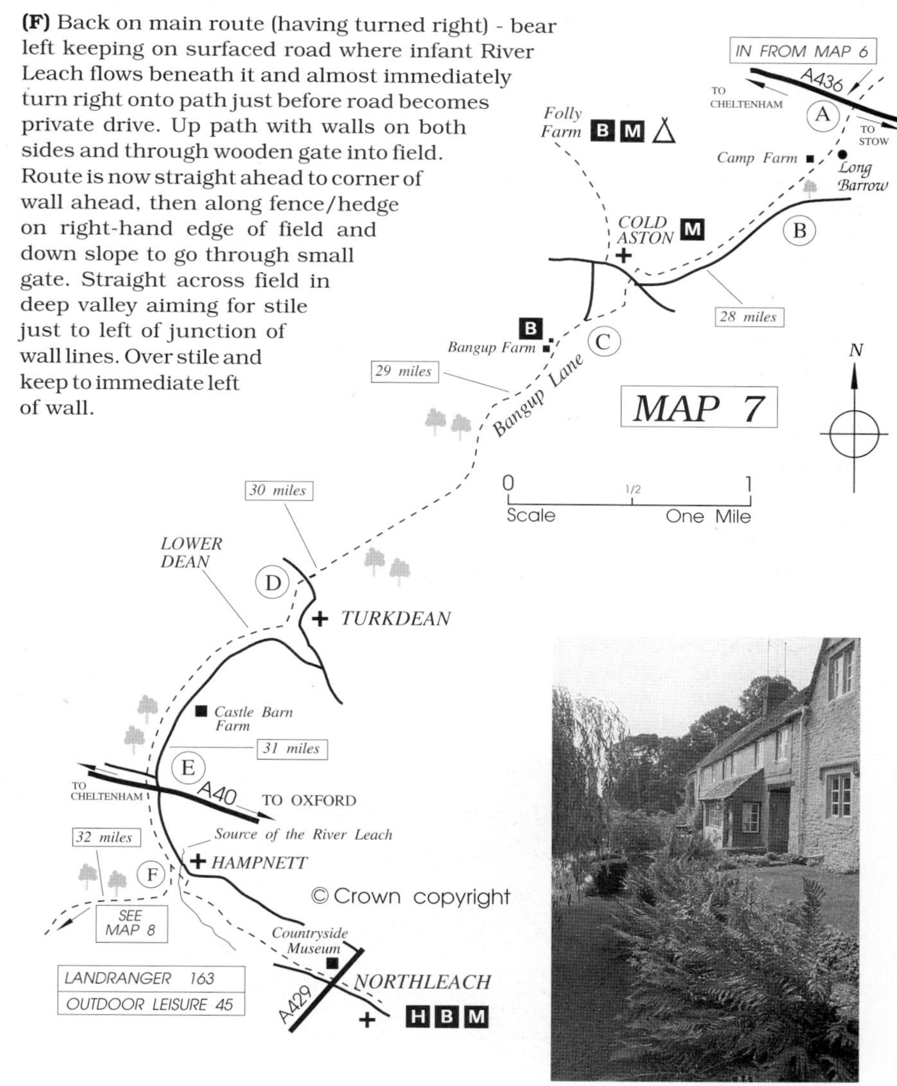

Cottages at Hampnett

(A) Through wooden gate and go across busy minor road onto smaller road forking right (SP - Fossebridge). After about 50 yards turn right down track with mature plantation on right and young plantation on left. Turn left at end of young plantation and note stone leaning against wall on immediate left beyond bend in wall. *This is known locally as the Hangman's Stone, and it appears to have been named as such due to a sheep-stealer who accidentally hung himself while getting over a stile in this wall with a stolen sheep in his arms. A highly moral, but rather unlikely story !* Now go into field keeping to immediate left of another young plantation on its right. Down field now keeping to immediate left of hedge and fence, soon veering slightly right and passing beneath electric power-line with large pylon just to right. Through gap in fence coming in from left into smaller field with large barns of Oxpens Farm on left. Soon turn left with fence and wall to immediate right and, just before reaching barns, turn right after stone wall.. Follow down between wall on right and fence with spinney on left and over stile. Go diagonally left across very small field.

(B) Soon turn right down well surfaced farm road and follow this down into valley. Cross stream, a tributary of River Coln and pass old, stone-lined sheep wash on right. Climb track up into farmyard, which marks our entry into Yanworth. Bend left and then right, following track through farmyard past attractive stone barns and, on right, delightful little Yanworth Church. *Here will be found a Norman south doorway, a chancel arch of the same period and a wall-painting of Old Father Time complete with his scythe.* Up surfaced road beyond church, turn left at top and almost immediately right onto road in village (SP - *Roman Villa*). Go through village, passing village hall on right, cast-iron water pump on left and delightful *Dolls' Cottage* and telephone box, both on right.

(C) Turn left at road junction (SP - *Fossebridge*) and go down road towards beautifully wooded Coln Valley. *Good view of fine Elizabethan mansion of Stowell Park well over to left.* Pass converted Yanworth Mill on right and, immediately beyond bridge over River Coln, turn right where road bends to left. Now on broad surfaced track with extensive woodlands up to left and water meadows to right as we walk parallel with River Coln. Many pheasants in woods - please keep dogs on lead.

(D) After one mile pass cottage on left and after another 200 yards go through gate to turn left onto surfaced road (SP - *Roman Villa*). Up fairly steep slope, keeping on surfaced road and ignoring track to left. Soon pass the National Trust's Chedworth Roman Villa on right and go onto footpath to immediate left of National Trust reception building. *In an attractive woodland setting and dating from between AD 180 and AD 350, these very interesting and beautifully preserved remains include bath suites, a hypocaust and mosaic pavements. There is also a museum and shop, and a 9-minute introductory film provides a fascinating insight into life and work in the Romano-British countryside. Don't miss a visit here - you could even reward yourself with an ice cream !* Go up steep, stony path through woods, soon disregarding steps up to left and going through underbridge beneath old railway

Chedworth Roman Villa

Woods beyond Chedworth Roman Villa

embankment. After 100 yards, turn left at x-rds of tracks and continue to climb up through woods. Straight, not right at junction of tracks, going onto possibly muddier track. Fork right at Y-junction of tracks going gently up hill.

(E) Over stile at end of wood and head straight across field to go to immediate right of fence coming in from left. Continue with fence now on immediate left, soon cross line of bridleway and through metal gate below sycamore tree. Go straight, not left, at next junction of paths and go steeply down through wood, initially on steps. Over stile at end of wood and keep in same direction across field in broad valley. Well concealed railway cutting beyond dense bushes to left, at southern end of old railway tunnel. Bear right near end of field and go over stile onto surfaced road at entry to Chedworth village. Soon pass church on right. *This light and airy building was considerably enriched in the Perpendicular period and has a stout Norman font, and, in contrast, an elegant 15th-century stone pulpit.* Keep on higher road (but bear left down path if you wish to visit the Seven Tuns, a welcoming inn with a spring bubbling out of a wall opposite). Pass attractive house and barn on right with pool in garden.

(F) Over first road and bear left up slope to left of village notice board. Immediately bear right across second road to go straight up track overhung with trees. After 100 yards, go straight over road onto track (SP - *Setts Farm House only*).

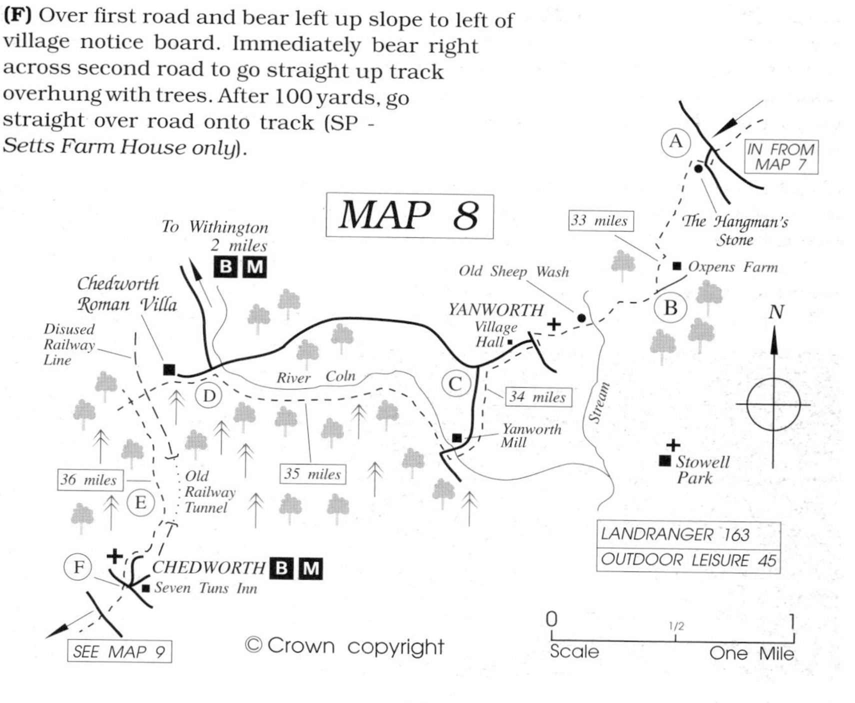

(A) At Setts Farm House keep on track through double wooden gates, then through two single gates and stay on this with open views ahead. Pass end of hedgeline on left and bear slightly left along track, with view ahead of 'restored' World War I airfield, known as 'RFC Rendcomb' (Strictly private - do not try to visit). Through wide gap in wall now following hedge on left and dropping gently into shallow valley. After about 200 yards, keep on track, leaving theoretical right-of-way and onto permissive section (not signed as such). Bear right in bottom of valley, keeping on track and soon turn left at junction of tracks ignoring tree-lined track ahead.

A hint of France at Rendcomb

(B) After about 200 yards turn right at junction of tracks, leaving permissive section and re-join right-of-way. Keep along broad track with open field on both sides, gradually rising out of valley. Through gap at end of track and turn left onto road which follows course of minor Roman road known as the White Way. Cross this road onto small lane to left of waymark to Greenmeadow Farm. Follow lane passing narrow strip of wood to left. Fine views of Rendcomb ahead including its 'chateau-style' stable-block tower. Down lane and up short, steep hill.

(C) Soon pass footpath to left. *Use this if you wish to divert to Cirencester down Churn Valley - five-and-a-half miles - using Map 9A. From Cirencester, use Map 9B to re-join the main route at the Tunnel House Inn (see Map 10, Point H) - a further three-and three-quarter miles). There would therefore be no extra mileage involved, as the total distance of this major diversion is the same as that between its starting and finishing points on the main route.* Back on main route just before entry to Rendcomb - turn left at road junction (phone box on left) by entry to estate village of Rendcomb, with Italianate Rendcomb Court used as boarding school. Pass Post Office shop and 'French-chateau-style' stable block (now school science building). Follow road to left. (But turn right if you wish to visit church.) *This was built by prosperous wool merchant, Sir Edmund Thame, son of the builder of better known Fairford church, with which it shares certain similarities. It also has a splendid Norman font.)* Follow road down hill, under bridge, cross infant River Churn and pass Rendcomb Surgery before reaching busy A435.

(D) Cross A435 with great care, going right and almost immediately left onto lane (SP - *Woodmancote*). Go up lane for at least half-a-mile, looking back for good view of Rendcomb College. Go left through large wooden gate opposite cottage named *The Lodge* and just before large pylon. Go diagonally across field heading for left-hand end of dutch barn. Go through metal gate to immediate left of dutch barn and follow short fence on right before passing cottage. Immediately beyond cottage go over stile to right. Follow track to road into quiet hamlet of Woodmancote.

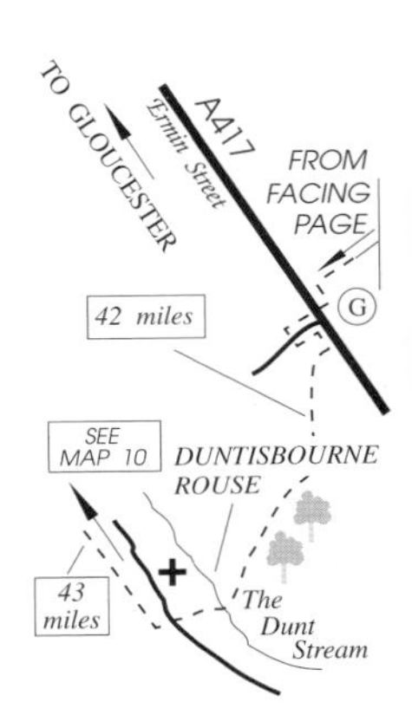

(E) Go left onto road in Woodmancote, telephone box soon on right by road junction. Bear right off road just beyond semi-detached house (*'No 2'*) on right and before sign *North Cerney* and onto short, sunken bridleway. At end of this go slightly left across junction of surfaced drives, and then bear

Duntisbourne Rouse Church (see page 32)

slightly right to go down lane passing just to right of Moor Wood, a large house with impressive gardens on both sides of lane. Keep on surfaced lane bearing slightly right to pass house with stables and cartshed just beyond on right. Keep down track with wood and stream on right.

(F) Soon fork left on track with hedge on left. Bend to left at valley bottom and climb up track with good views back across valley to Woodmancote, to pass coniferous wood on left. After one-third-of-a-mile go straight ahead on concrete drive towards house near Dartley Farm, but just before house go left onto tarmac lane leading to embanked A417 road (*This follows the course of the Romans' Ermin Way, which ran from Silchester, near Reading, through Cirencester, to their legionary fortress at Gloucester).*

(G) Bear round to left where farm road becomes concreted and go through small wooden gate. Turn right, onto minor road and under two bridges beneath A417. About 150 paces beyond 2nd bridge, turn sharp left, through small wooden gate to go back on yourself along farm road between wooden fences. Soon bear right to go parallel with A417 and then turn right through double metal gates. Go along edge of field with hedge on left before turning left through metal gate. Now go immediately right with bushy hedge now on right and, after a while, through next metal gate keeping hedge on right. Cirencester Park woodlands visible ahead. Continue skirting right-hand edge of field before bearing off right, out of field at bottom corner to go down path between hedge on right and wood on left. Continue down sunken lane and go over small bridge to left of ford crossing the Dunt stream in Duntisbourne Rouse hamlet.
(Now turn to page 32)

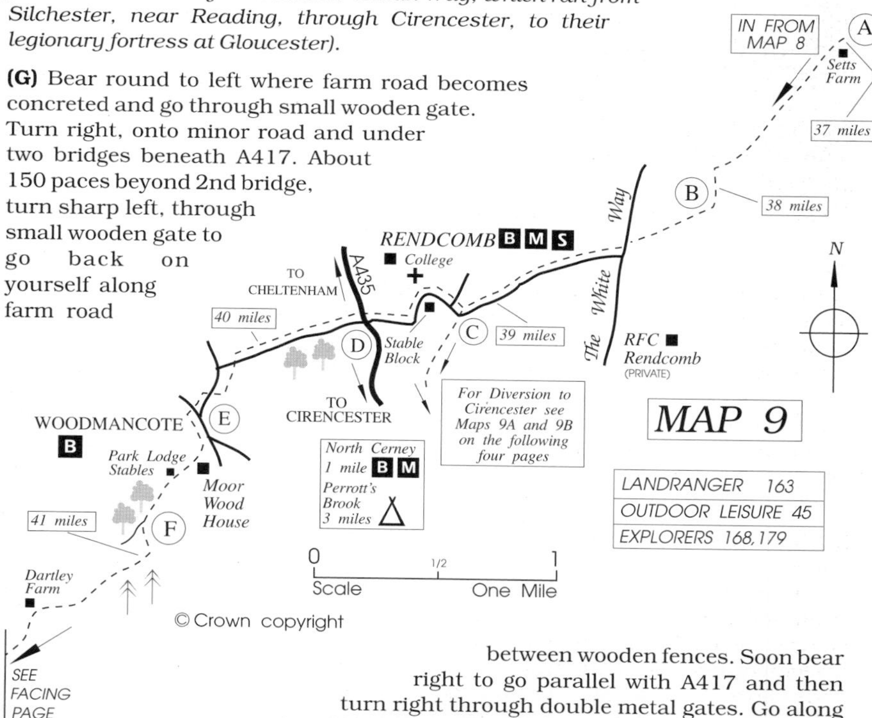

The Cirencester Diversion - Part 1

The River Churn, near North Cerney

(A) Leave Main Route at Map 9, Point C, by turning left off road at top of slope just before entering Rendcomb. Go along top of field with fence to immediate right, keep in same line beyond fence'e end and through iron kissing gate. Continue at same angle across track and follow sign down into narrow wood. Soon through kissing gate, turn left into field and follow round it keeping fenced edge of wood on immediate left. Over stile, cross main track and go through small coniferous plantation to hunting gate into field, ignoring footpath sign up to right. Walk along pleasant meadow parallel with River Churn to right. At end of field, ignore footbridge to right, and go through hunting gate just beyond. Along winding track through next field with meandering Churn to right. Near end of field through gateway gap in wall over to left and bear half-left up track. After three small trees on right bear right off defined track and follow along top of steep slope coming up from right. Aim towards Cedar of Lebanon beyond house ahead and soon through large wooden gate at entry to North Cerney.

(B) Turn left onto road by phone box and immediately fork right (SP - *Calmsden*) *(but turn right if you wish to visit Bathurst Arms or church)*. Bear right up hill and almost immediately turn right off road and through wooden gate by transformer on poles. Good view of church over to right. After few yards turn left over stile and continue in same direction with fence on immediate right. Through squeeze stile beside hunting gate and follow to immediate left of fence beyond farm on right. Through large wooden gate into next field and follow right-hand edge of field with fence to right. Ignore bridge to right and through hunting gate, keeping to bottom of field with line of willows to right. Through large wooden gate and onto track with fence on left and hedge on right. Onto surfaced driveway at Perrott's Brook Farm with houses first on right and then on left. Keep straight down driveway passing barns on left and then bear right onto road.

(C) At road junction by Perrott's Brook entry sign go straight across road and bear left onto track in woodland carpeted with bluebells and other small flowers in spring *(but turn right if you wish to visit the Bear Inn - visible from here)*. Leave wood beyond small building on left and follow track along right-hand edge of field. Through wooden gate and continue across meadow in same direction. Passing beneath bypass viaduct. Where meadow narrows, bear slightly left up

St John's Hospital, Cirencester

path onto bank to keep in same direction through scrubby area. Through wooden gate and metal gate and onto track with beech hedge to left and small stream to right.

(D) Bear left at junction of tracks and onto surfaced road at entry to Baunton. Pass Baunton church on right. *Do try to visit this, to look at the unique 14th-century wall-painting of St Christopher.* Go straight across at road junction in Baunton, pass phone box on left and go round to right at T-junction. Bear left off road by Manor Farm onto surfaced track and soon through metal gate and then through wooden gate. Soon over stile and across large field aiming for centre of wood ahead, but keeping to left of minor stream and of fragmented hedge extending from wood. Over small stile beside horse-jump and up short, steep path into wood. Soon bear right onto well-defined path along woodland slope before bearing up left to go over stile at end of wood. Across field aiming for power pole to left of tower of Cirencester Church. At end of field, ignore footpath waymark ahead and branch slightly left through gateway to follow parallel bridleway.

(E) Through metal gate just before Bowling Green Farm and keep onto surfaced roadway into outskirts of Cirencester passing house on left called 'Meadow View'. Keep straight along Bowling Green Lane **to go over Cirencester's inner bypass with very great care**. Pass phone box on left, over small bridge crossing River Churn and head towards Post Office Stores. Turn left into Gloucester Street by stores and Nelson Inn. Over x-rds into Dollar Street *(but turn left if you wish to look at the beautiful arcading of St John's Hospital, which was founded by Henry II).*

(F) Pass north side of Cirencester Parish Church on left and bear left into Market Place beyond church's west end.

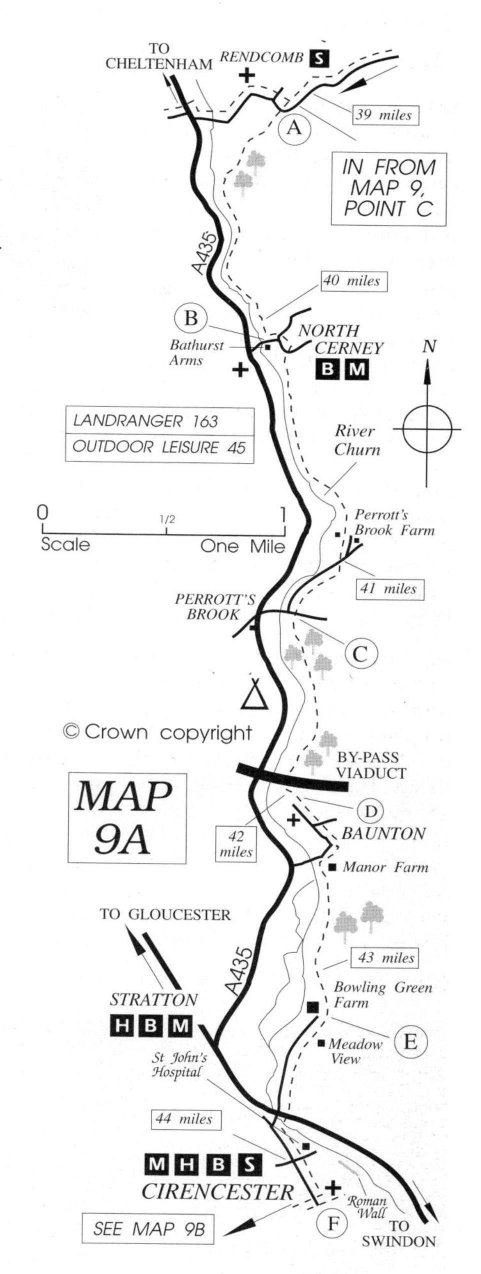

The Cirencester Diversion - Part 2

This busy market town stands on the site of Corinium Dobunnorum and was for a time Roman Britain's second largest city and meeting point of three major Roman roads. It remains today the undisputed centre of life and work in the southern Cotswolds and offers all that the Cross-Cotswold Pathway user requires in the way of shops, B&Bs, hotels, eating places and helpful TIC. Near our entry to the town are the surviving arcades of St John's Hospital, but most visitors will head for the Market Place, which is overlooked by Cirencester's fine Parish Church. This was generously endowed with the wealth of the town's wool merchants and has a magnificent 162-ft Perpendicular tower, a massive three-storeyed south porch and an equally impressive interior. The turf-covered Roman amphitheatre lies to the south of the ring road and on the other side of the town there is a stretch of Roman city wall to the east of the delightful Abbey Grounds. The fascinating Corinium Museum has one of Britain's best collections of Romano-british material and is well worth visiting. To the right of our route out of the town lies the great expanse of Cirencester Park, with its Broad Ride stretching westwards to Sapperton, almost five miles away.

(A) Head southwards from the Market Place, go along Castle Street and over road at end onto Fosse Way. Head out of town on Fosse Way passing Bridges Garage on left and **going over Stroud Road with great care** by large roundabout onto A429. After 350 yards turn right off road beyond house on right opposite haulage depot and onto footpath going diagonally left across field with young trees. On reaching hedgeline bear left and soon go onto tarmac pathway keeping to immediate right of all-weather games pitch. Follow tarmac path, pass sports pavilion on right and cross main drive to Royal Agricultural College (up to right).

Keep to left-hand edge of playing field, through wooden gate and down grassy track with hedges on both sides. Through squeeze stile to left of wooden gate and down track in same direction *(track up to left leads to College Farm)*. Straight, not right, at junction of tracks in valley. Out of valley on grassy track and beyond farm buildings and house on left (Field Barn) bear right onto surfaced track with fence to left. After 200 yards turn left over stile by beech tree and follow left-hand edge of field. Turn right in first corner of field and keep to left-hand edge of field with woodland to left. Through gate just to right of field corner and keep in same direction down left-hand edge of next field.

Cirencester Church

(B) Over two stiles crossing narrow belt of woodland and keep in same direction along left-hand edge of next field, eventually passing pool beyond hedge to left. Handsome 18th-century Bledisloe Lodge visible over to right. Over stile on left and turn right to continue in same direction within very narrow, young plantation. Pass Fosse Hill House on left and soon cross minor road and over small ladder stile across wall. Follow down two fields with fence to

The Tunnel House Inn, near Coates

immediate left and parkland of Trewsbury House up to left within earthworks of large Iron Age hill fort (not very apparent). Over stile and keep in same line but now with fence to right.

(C) Through metal gate, turn left onto track over old canal bridge and immediately turn right to go onto towpath to left of overgrown canal bed - the remains of the Thames and Severn Canal (see page 34). *(But turn right again, go under bridge and along towpath for half a mile if you wish to visit Thames Head - the official and often dry, source of the River Thames - and possibly link to head of Thames Path (see page 34).* After half a mile, go under railway bridge and pass ruined 18th-century Gothick canal round house. After 400 yards, go under road bridge and continue along towpath, now beside a water-filled section of canal to arrive at eastern portal of canal tunnel and Tunnel House Inn, thereby rejoining main route at Map 10, Point H.

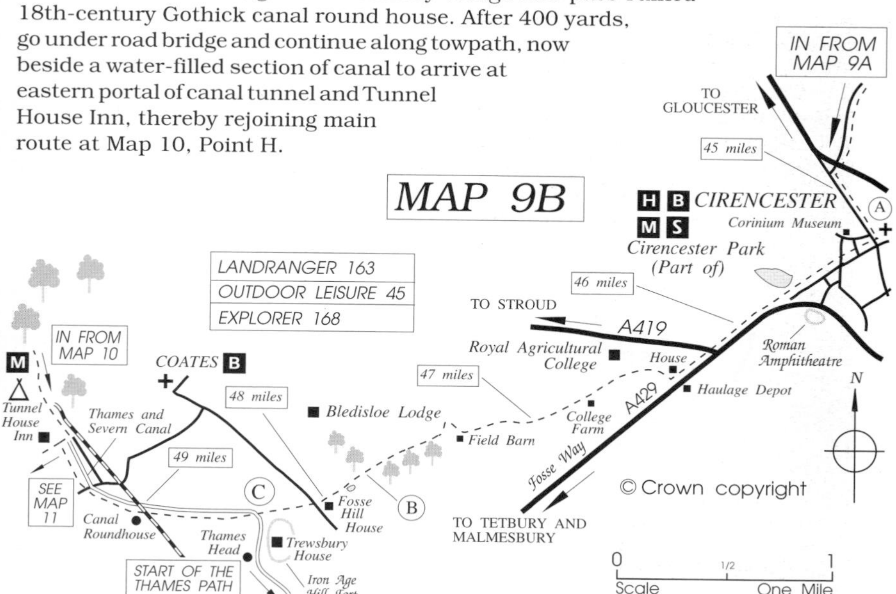

(Continued from Page 27)

(A) Go up short lane and turn right onto minor road (SP - *The Duntisbournes / Youth Hostel*). After 100 yards pass entry to exceptionally interesting Duntisbourne Rouse church on right - don't miss a visit. *This tiny Saxon church has a saddleback roof to its tower and an interior complete with box pews, carved misericords to its choir stalls and medieval wall paintings on its north chancel wall. Being built on a slope it has, most unusually, a little crypt beneath its eastern end.* After about 300 yards turn left onto bridleway. Go along bridleway and after 300 yards bear right by wooden barn on left and follow track to right.

(B) After three-quarters-of-a-mile, cross minor road and through wooden gate onto further bridleway, which skirts to right (north) of Overley Wood - the northern fringe of Cirencester Park's great woodlands. *Please note that almost all the way from here to the Tunnel House Inn (see opposite) is within Cirencester Park, part of the Bathurst Estate, and to meet this estate's requirements, Macmillan Way waymarks will unfortunately not be displayed. However, the route is well signed with standard waymarks and little difficulty should be experienced.* At end of bridleway turn left onto minor road and pass Gloucester Lodge on left - this is one of the northern entrances to Cirencester Park. Continue southwards on minor road.

(C) Immediately after passing signed entrance to Pinbury Park (private) turn right onto bridleway and immediately right again through hunting gate. Follow an indistinct path on immediate right of hawthorn hedge and parallel with private road to Pinbury Park on right. Veer to left as bridleway drops down to run close to private road. Soon leave private road and skirt to left of pond, going between pond and its feeding spring. Through double gates just beyond pond and follow field path south-westwards aiming between two power-poles. *Lovely 17th-century Pinbury Park (house) visible back across valley to right.*

(D) Through gate into bushy area and at junction of tracks just beyond, carry straight ahead, slightly up hill, ignoring path to left. Continue south-westwards on path in middle of delightful meadow ringed by fine trees. Through gate keeping on path to left of fence with view of house called *The Leasowes* to right. Continuing left, pass through small gate and turn right onto well defined bridleway. Through gate and bear half-left to cross field to telephone box in Sapperton village. *Sapperton church is over to right and is approached down a path below yew trees. In the north transept of this largely 18th-century building. Sir Henry Poole, who died in 1616, lies in a great canopied Renaissance tomb, with many effigies. Adjacent to it is another Poole tomb dated 1574. In the south transept Sir Robert Atkyns, who died in 1711, lies on his left elbow with his hand resting upon a book. He was the county historian and wrote* 'The Ancient and Present State of Gloucestershire'. *Trim and colourful Sapperton is very much a Bathurst estate village and below it, runs the tunnel of the two-and-a-quarter-mile-long Thames and Severn Canal (see page 34), the western portal of which is at Daneway in the valley below Sapperton.*

Sapperton Church

(E) Back on main route - turn left up hill near telephone box, soon passing the Bell Inn on left and bus stop. Turn right at road junction (SP - *Cherington*) and soon cross 'The Sapperton Broad Avenue', *a broad grassy ride, also known as 'The Broad Ride', which runs eastwards for nearly five miles to Cirencester, with only a short break in open country around Pope's Seat. A notice states 'You are welcome on horseback or on foot* *along the Sapperton Broad Avenue. Please keep dogs on leads'. It should be noted however that this facility applies only between 8 am and 5pm.*

(F) Soon turn left at x-rds (SP - *Cirencester*). Go along road, with view to right of one of the spoil heaps created by the excavators of the tunnel for the Thames and Severn Canal. Ignore first fingerpost to right and **proceed with great care along this often busy minor road** until a plantation joins our road on left. At this point turn right, off road and through gap in stone wall. Cross field, through large metal gates and **cross busy A419 with great care** to go through more large metal gates. Continue in same direction across field noting another tunnel spoil heap over to right.

(G) At end of field go through gate into Hailey Wood and continue ahead veering slightly left on track to plunge into this very large wood. Continue on track ignoring other crossing rides and paths and approximately following the course of canal tunnel beneath. *Note spoil heap to right (not easy to to spot in summer) with exposed air shaft,* ***but keep away from fenced edge - it could be very dangerous****. Like the rest, this shaft was first used to extract spoil from the tunnel beneath and was then used for ventilation.* After about 500 yards veer slightly to left and soon go straight across wide track which descends from estate saw-mill up to left (not visible) and which also goes to right, over embankment, with parapet of railway bridge just visible beyond. Continue on footpath, then turn half-right at junction with track coming in from left. Go under railway line, turn left and follow path running parallel with railway, and pass through gate before reaching vicinity of Tunnel House Inn.

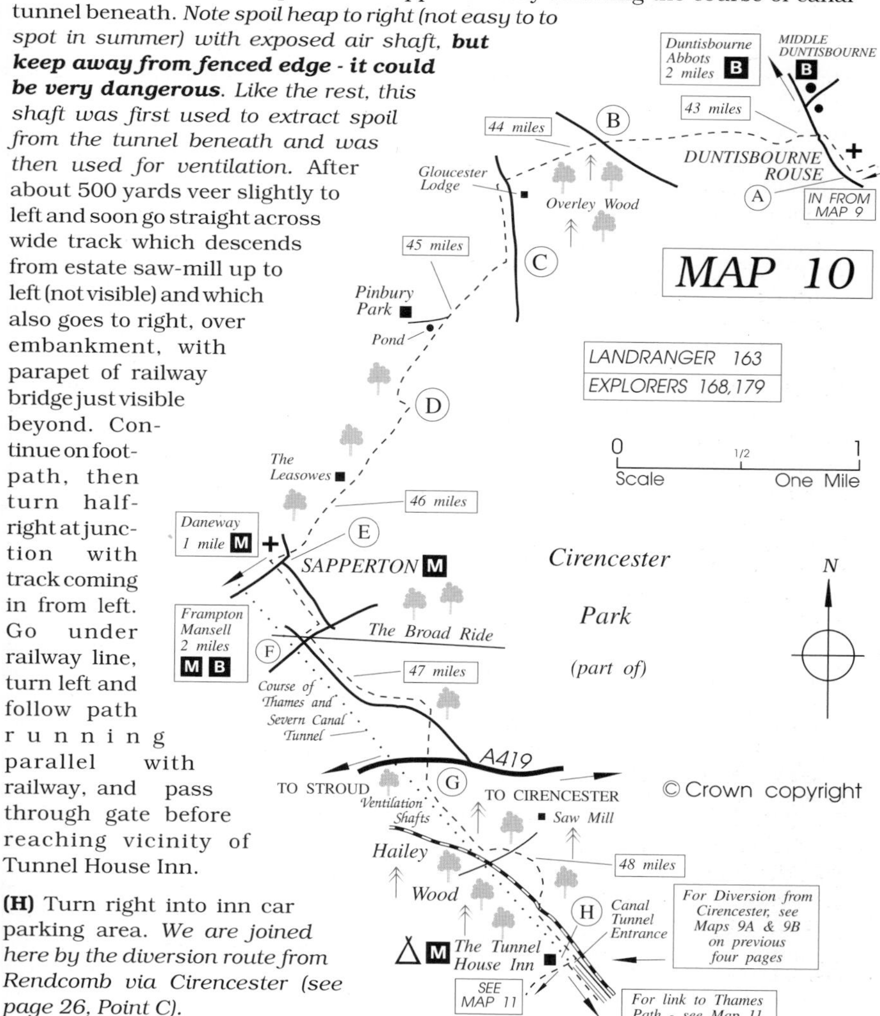

(H) Turn right into inn car parking area. *We are joined here by the diversion route from Rendcomb via Cirencester (see page 26, Point C).*

Chapter 3 Tunnel House Inn, Coates - Bath

38 Miles

(A) Go through car parking area in front of Tunnel House Inn and between inn and low building to its left, passing old cider press on left, going down to gap in wall. *(However, follow towpath along bank of partly restored Thames and Severn Canal if you wish to link onto the Thames Path at Thames Head, the source of the Thames, which is about a mile away.) The Tunnel House Inn was built to house, feed and especially water, the navvies who dug the canal tunnel and the thirsty boatmen who used it when completed. The tunnel, the delightful portal of which is still visible near the inn, was completed in 1789 and was, at that time, the longest canal tunnel in England. It enabled boats to cross the Cotswolds from the head of the navigable Thames at Lechlade to the Severn via the Stroudwater Canal. Sadly it was finally abandoned in 1927. Now an attractive and welcoming pub, the Tunnel House is full of curiosities and delights. Chris Keyte, the landlord, has very kindly offered to make a pound donation to Macmillan Cancer Relief for every group of Macmillan sponsored walkers who sign the Visitors Book. Don't miss a call here - its a great pub.*

(B) Now back on main route beyond Tunnel House Inn, having gone through gap in wall beyond cider press. Go along wide footpath through field, *with very slight earthworks of Roman 'settlement' sometimes visible over to left. Now known as Tunnel Mouth Camp it was probably a religious complex dating from the 3rd or 4th century AD, but it has never been systematically excavated (Do not Trespass).* Over stone stile in wall into next field and now follow line of power-poles, which presently leads towards stile in cross-wall ahead. Over this stile and up across next field to go through small gate beside stile. Go diagonally right, across field to fingerpost and through metal gate near small house in Tarlton.

(C) At entry to Tarlton, *a minute village with a number of pleasant houses and a small neo-Norman church*, go slightly left, cross road and turn right onto well surfaced track leading through farmyard. Pass converted barns on right and walk through farmyard to leave Tarlton on track beyond farm cottages on right. Bear slightly left keeping on farm track and after about half-a-mile, at end of track, go through metal gate into field. Turn half right to cross corner of field and through second metal gate. Keep in same direction across corner of next field to go through third metal gate and across larger field aiming to right of tall trees in line of woodland ahead. Go through wooden gate into scrubby woodland. Now veer slightly left to follow very short track.

(D) Soon turn left onto surfaced track and head south-westwards with woodlands to left. After about 600 yards go straight ahead to join minor road. After about 50 yards go straight ahead onto track where road turns left. After just over half a mile cross minor road and through wooden gate onto further track in same direction.

(E) After about 350 yards and at first wall-line to right, turn right through old, small gateway *(now on permissive path - Macmillan Way and Cross-Cotswold Pathway walkers only)* and go up right-hand side of field keeping wall on immediate right. At end of field bear slightly right through gap and bear slightly left joining farm track. Drop down on track bearing left at bottom with good view of delightful

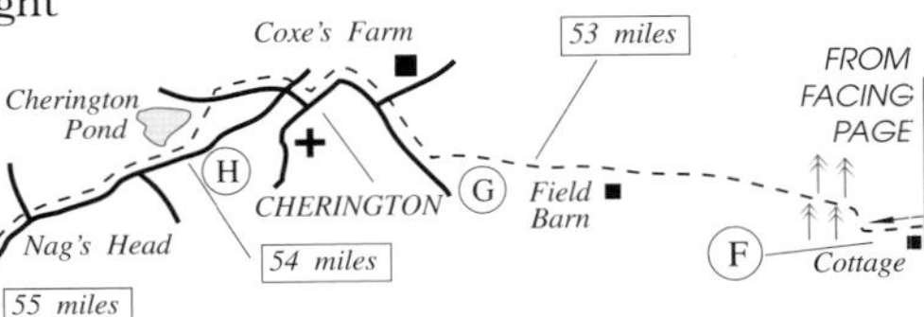

East Portal of the Thames and Severn Canal Tunnel

16th- and 17th-century Hazleton Manor over to left. Bear left at junction of tracks and keep on track out of small valley (do not go through gates into field to right). Now bear right, then left, with barns to left. Turn right just beyond transformer on pole to left *(re-joining normal right-of-way)* and go straight along farm road to Shepherd's Cottages.

(F) At end of farm road go straight across field to gate. Through this gate into wood and after about 20 yards, fork right along waymarked pathway (yellow arrows only). Soon bear left and after going along narrow path, emerge at end of wood. Now follow right-hand field boundaries to go across five fields in a straight line, passing Field Barn on left and keeping to immediate left of hedgelines where they exist.

(G) Through gap beside metal gate, bear right onto public road and go straight, not right by Coxe's Farm at entry to Cherington village (SP - *Avening*). Turn right (SP - *Avening*) by pleasant green *overlooked by several attractive 18th and early 19th-century cottages, with an ancient wellhead on it, inscribed, 'Let Him that is athirst, come'. The nearby church is largely 13th-century in origin and has a Norman south doorway with tympanum, a Norman tub font and a list of rectors, curates and patrons dating back to 1287.* Just beyond village, go over diagonal x-rds roads on hill (SP - *Stroud*) and **go down steep hill with care**. At bottom of hill bear left off road by parking space and through wooden gate. Keep on often muddy path with stream on right and pass delightful lake on right, known as Cherington Pond. At end of lake bear left up slight incline.

(H) Soon through small wooden gate and bear right onto minor road. Keep on road through hamlet of Nag's Head (the pub has gone long ago), keeping straight, not right by telephone box. After 500 yards go straight, not left and after further 300 yards, turn left onto busier road into Avening village (SP - *Tetbury*).

MAP 11
IN FROM MAP 10
Course of Canal Tunnel
Tunnel Entrance
Coates 1 mile B
Tunnel House Inn
For Diversion from Cirencester, see Maps9 A & 9B
Tunnel Mouth Camp
Canal Roundhouse
Bed of Thames and Severn Canal
Source of the River Thames
50 miles
49 miles
51 miles
52 miles
TARLTON
Rodmarton 1 mile B
To Kemble Station 2 miles
LANDRANGER 162,163
EXPLORER 168
SEE FACING PAGE
Hazleton Manor
N
0 1/2 1
Scale One Mile

(A) After 200 yards pass Cross Inn on left and go straight onto B4014 (SP - *Nailsworth*), passing small general stores on left. After 200 yards bear left up Point Road by telephone box. Soon keep straight, **not** left up Pound Hill, but descend, with good view of Avening church down to right and then bear left at T-junction and up hill, still on Point Road. Straight, not left at road junction by de-restriction signs (SP - *West End*) and just beyond, turn left through large wooden gate, up a steep grassy footpath. Over stile (good views back over valley to Gatcombe Park) and walk as near as possible to right-hand edge of field. Keep to right of small spinney near right-hand edge of field and over stone stile. Follow wall to left soon passing fine farmhouse on left with clock tower.

(B) Over stile to left of metal gate, cross surfaced farm drive, then over horse-jump and along next field keeping wall on left. Over rudimentary stile and continue with wall still on left, but just before end of field, bear left over massive stone stile and go diagonally left across field aiming for far left-hand corner just to right of clump of trees. Go through gap, turn left through second gap and immediately right onto B4014 road. Go along road and after 200 yards, at first gentle bend to left, bear right through gap. Then turn left into spinney and immediately go diagonally right aiming just to left of pylon, and then for footpath sign. Over stone stile, cross minor road and over rudimentary stile in wall. Go diagonally right, across field aiming for wall heading straight towards you at far side. Through large gap in cross-hedge and into next field keeping to immediate right of parallel wall. Over rudimentary stile in left-hand end of cross-fence near end of field.

(C) Soon go through gate to cross minor road. *(But walk about 100 yards down road to left for glimpse of Chavenage House through its entrance gates.) Chavenage is a delightful Elizabethan manor house, which was once visited by Oliver Cromwell, to persuade the owner, Colonel Nathaniel Stephens, to put his name to Charles I's Death Warrant. The colonel grudgingly agreed, but then died within three months of the king's execution, apparently full of remorse.*

(C) On main route - over road going slightly right, onto farm road with asbestos barn to right and old stone barn to left. Bear slightly left down sometimes muddy bridleway (known as Chavenage Lane) going between walls, soon passing wood on left, rich with bluebells in late spring. At end of wood, go down bridleway bordered by hedges and trees.

(D) Through gate, bear down left and through another gate at bottom of small valley. *If you wish to divert to Tetbury for overnight stop, fork left onto path along valley (probably not waymarked) keeping low wall on left. Bear left over stile at end of wall and along often muddy, ill-defined path in wooded area. Keep parallel with field on right. Turn right onto lane and in a few yards bear left at road junction. Soon enter Tetbury - under two miles. This unspoilt little market town is centred upon its delightful 17th-century Market House and the nearby church of St Mary. But in addition to these main features, Tetbury has a wealth of interesting old buildings and is well worth visiting. To return to main route - leave centre of town on Church Street, turn right into West Street, opposite church and then bear left down Cotton's Lane. Soon turn left onto Cutwell and cross River Avon on small stone bridge beside ford. Turn right onto Longfurlong Lane and leave town on this, keeping straight not right well beyond. At end of Longfurlong Lane, go through two gates in front of Elmestree Lodge. Now go diagonally left across fields and parkland in front of Elmestree*

Tetbury Church

House following waymarks. Slight hint of Highgrove House over to left. Then into another field with hedge on left before going on grassy gallop for short distance. Then bear left over stile through hedge and follow in same direction along three fields, keeping to immediate left of hedge-line. Now over final stile and re-join main route at Point G (see below) by turning left onto Hookshouse Lane, some 400 yards north of diagonal x-rds near Westonbirt. (Distance from Tetbury under three miles)

(D) Back on main route, in valley beyond Chavenage. Aim slightly left and go up slope with fence and bushes to right, with good view back to Chavenage House. Through large metal gate at top of slope and continue on bridleway with hedge to right. Fine distant views to left of Tetbury with its splendid, tall-spired church. Continue on bridleway with good views of Beverston Castle over to right before reaching A4135.

(E) Turn right onto often busy A4135 and almost immediately turn left off it through hunting gate beside large metal gates. *(But follow road westwards for half-a-mile if you wish to visit Beverston. The church in this small village has an unusual Anglo-Saxon sculpture on its tower and some interesting features within. Beverston Castle, one of the few surviving Cotswold castles, is nearby, a largely 13th-century building with 17th-century additions. It is not open but glimpses can be obtained from the road.)* On main route - follow broad and grassy bridleway, eventually going onto more defined track with trees and fences on both sides, and into small valley. Up track beyond it and through field before going through gate and bearing right at Hookshouse hamlet.

(F) Almost immediately fork left at road junction by interesting Hookshouse Pottery on right (SP - *Westonbirt*). Follow Hookshouse Lane southwards passing Charlton Down (house) on left.

(G) After about half-a-mile pass footpath sign on left *(this is where diversion route from Tetbury rejoins main route)*.

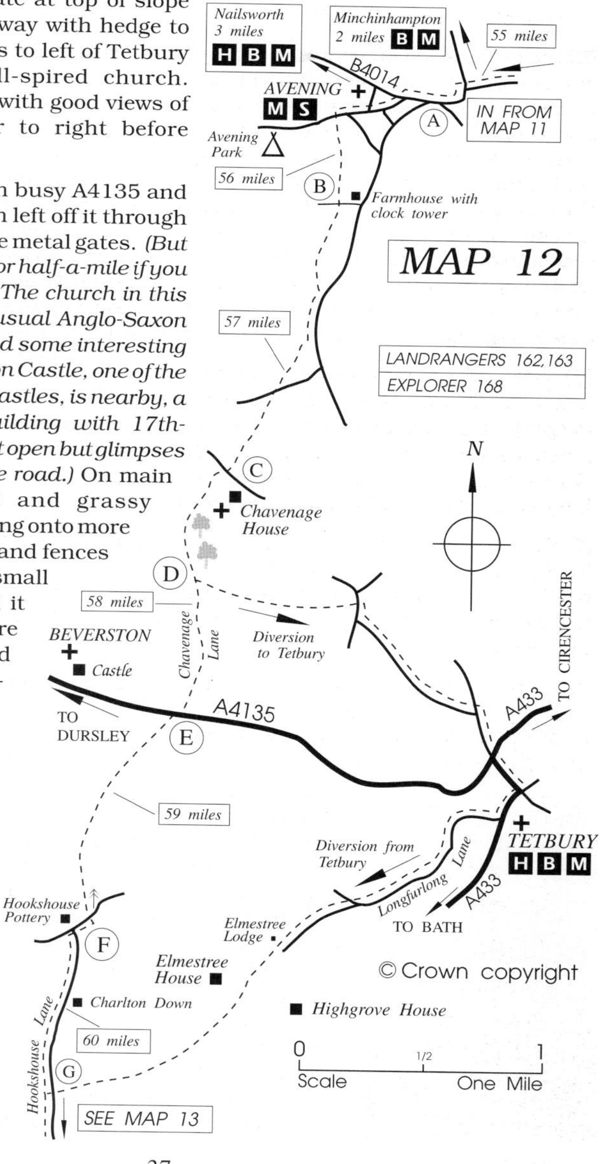

(A) At diagonal x-rds turn right over stile and along field with wall on immediate right. Through gate and keep to left-hand edge of field with northern edge of Westonbirt Arboretum to left - occasional vistas of tall and exotic trees, undulating lawns, leisurely seats and arbours. Through gate into next field, still following wall on left. Down Farm visible over to right with the Beaufort Polo Club's pavilion to its immediate right. Through offset gap in wooden fence and through two more gates continuing on same line.

(B) Just before spinney, visible ahead, go through gate on left into Arboretum's field. Descend this field on sunken cart track, then veer slightly right in small valley and go over squeeze stile (ignoring standard waymarks) on edge of wood (now on a Permissive Path). *But turn left down valley and purchase entry tickets at far end of car park if you wish to leave course of Macmillan Way and visit rest of Arboretum, with its Visitor Centre, cafe and shop.) Westonbirt Arboretum was the creation of Sir Robert Holford, the owner of nearby neo-Elizabethan Westonbirt House, which is now a school. This world famous collection of over 13,000 trees stands in a beautiful 600-acre landscape with woodland paths and grassy glades. It has been owned by the Forestry Commission since 1956.* Back on main route - over squeeze stile into Westonbirt Arboretum's Silk Wood and bear slightly to right before going left up slope. At top of bank go over well defined path, bearing very slightly right, passing waymark post. Go along well defined grassy ride to next post beneath beech tree. Bear very slightly left aiming for next post and here, veer very slightly right to arrive at post beneath large pine tree. Here vere slightly left to head for next post where you turn 90 degrees left to follow path out of trees, down grassy slope to left of small clump of trees.

(C) At junction of drives keep in same direction down the Broad Drive, the main north-south axis of the Silk Wood. Keep in same direction, ignoring paths to left and right and aiming for large gate in distance. Go through hunting gate beside large gate, which marks southern extremity of Silk Wood *(but turn right (SP - Willow Collection), along path just within wood if you wish to go to Avenue Farm for B&B).* On main route, cross field keeping to immediate left of hedge.

(D) Through metal gate, **cross busy A433 with great care**, passing from Gloucestershire into Wiltshire and going onto wide track (Wood Lane) between house on left and kennels on right (beware of dog droppings). Through gate into next field keeping hedge on immediate left. Tower of Sherston church already visible well ahead, with distant Marlborough Downs on skyline well to its left. Follow path to end of field and through gate to cross very narrow field with barn to right. Soon pass beneath ash trees and into next field keeping on track with hedge to immediate right.

(E) Through gate at end of field and continue in same direction down road. Soon pass Halfway Bush Farm on right. Pass one new cross-wall on left and 100 yards beyond, go through gate on left. Go diagonally right, across field to far corner aiming for farm buildings well beyond. Bear right in corner through metal gate and along left-hand edge of field with hedge and wall on left. Through gap in cross hedge and continue in same line with hedge still on left. At end of field go straight ahead onto wide track with hedge on left and wall on right. Sherston visible over to right and house to left.

The Broad Drive, Westonbirt Arboretum

(F) Turn right onto road but immediately over stile and cross field to kissing gate in wall with Sherston church tower visible ahead. Through kissing gate and follow well used path to another kissing gate. Up driveway with houses on right and wall on left at entry to Sherston and bear right onto B4040. *A large village with wide main street, Sherston was a borough by the 15th century and the variety of beautiful stone houses and inns still bear witness to its past prosperity. Only just over the border into Wiltshire, but it already seems to have a slightly 'West Country' flavour, with several inns offering food and a number of shops. Its church has a handsomely vaulted Perpendicular porch and a stout tower, surprisingly built as late as 1730.* Walk through Sherston on B4040, passing Carpenters Arms on left and church on right. Pass Rattlebone Inn on left, Post Office on right and phone box on left. After passing Platts Stores on left, **take care when walking down steep road with dangerously blind bend**.

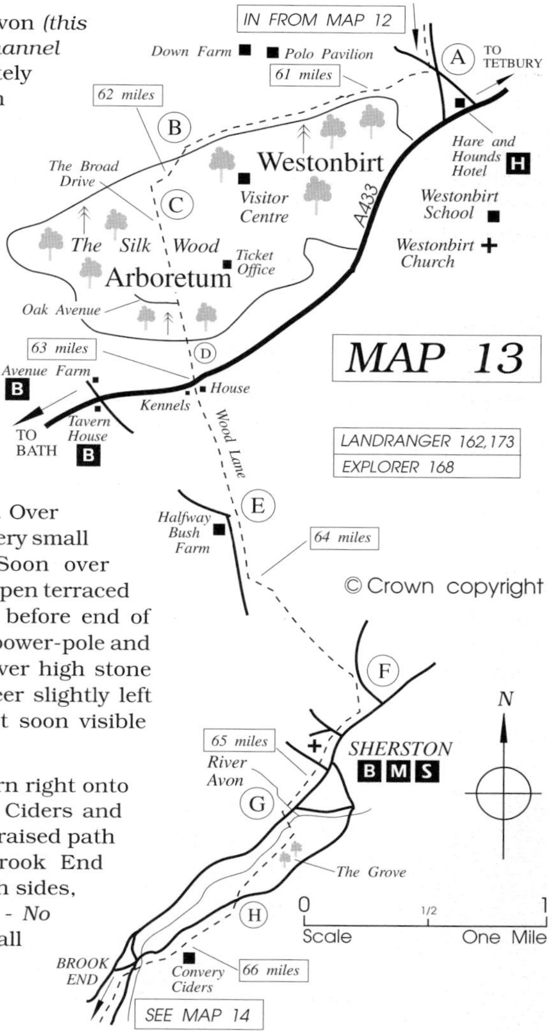

(G) Soon cross infant River Avon *(this one flows into the Bristol Channel at Avonmouth)* and immediately beyond, go over stone stile on left (SP - *The Grove*). *In the event of flooding in field ahead, turnabout, soon fork right and take first four turns to right, to use minor roads to rejoin route near Convery Ciders - see below.* On main route - bear right beyond stile aiming for bridge in field. Over bridge crossing tributary of River Avon, continue in same direction with stream now on right and wooded area known as 'The Grove' to left. Over stile and go straight across very small field dotted with scrub. Soon over another stile and into large open terraced field. Go along terrace but before end of field veer up left just before power-pole and up onto top terrace to go over high stone stile in left-hand corner. Veer slightly left and head for waymark post soon visible across field.

(H) Over stile in wall and turn right onto road. Pass sign to Convery Ciders and Wines on left and soon over raised path beside ford at entry to Brook End hamlet. After houses on both sides, turn left at offset x-rds (SP - *No Through Road*) to go down small lane with pleasant old houses on both sides. Go along raised path beside another ford (on left) before going on gravel track.

(A) Bear up right towards stable yard at entry to Luckington, but just before entrance gates with small lions, go through gap in wall to their left and onto path through churchyard, keeping to right of church and noting signs warning of falling masonry. *The church is a modest building of 13th-century origin with some handsome 18th-century tomb chests in its churchyard. It has a delightful neighbour in Luckington Court, a mellow and beautifully proportioned Queen Anne house.* Through front gate of churchyard onto tarmac path leading to another gate onto road. Turn right onto road, immediately pass entrance to Luckington Court on right and after a few yards turn left and over stile onto path between two houses *(but go straight ahead up road if you wish to visit the Old Royal Ship Inn, or village shop).* Soon over stile into field, first following hedge on right and then diagonally right aiming for electricity pole and going through gap in hedge. Now bear left to go diagonally to far bottom corner of field. Over wooden stile and follow winding path down into more wooded area. Over bridge crossing stream and turn right to go along valley bottom, with willow-bordered stream now to right, and head for gate.

(B) Through gate, turn right onto minor road. Immediately before road junction, turn left off road and go over small stile in wall to left of gate. Go up grounds of bungalow keeping close to wall on left and to left of two outbuildings. Over stile into small paddock and over second stile into large field. Continue in same line (southwards) keeping to left-hand edge of field with hedge on left. Go through very wide gap in partial cross hedge.

(C) Continue into field in same direction for about 200 yards before veering right (south-westwards) to aim for ash tree in middle of facing hedge. Through waymarked gap in hedge to right of ash tree and continue in same direction, diagonally across next field aiming for far right-hand top corner. Keep to immediate left of small triangular plantation and near corner of field through squeeze-stile in thick hedge. Keeping in same direction, go diagonally left across small field aiming for waymarked stile in hedge. Over this stile and go across next field passing well to left of small pond (with Hebden Farm visible over to right) to go through large metal gate. Note old brick-kiln over to right just beyond small house.

(D) Bear left beyond gate (now southwards) aiming to left of bushes which surround a larger, partly concealed, pond. Over stile by gateway to left of pond and veer slightly right aiming for point between two oaks in valley. Soon over two small concrete 'bridges' and through underbridge in railway embankment carrying busy Swindon - Bristol line **(Do not attempt to cross railway line, which is used by many very fast trains)**. Now head up towards lone oak tree in large meadow and then to right-hand end of wood on left.

Remains of Lugbury Long Barrow

(E) Through gateway at end of wood on left and veer slightly left aiming for gate well to left of extensive woodlands ahead. Through gate and veer left to cross small part of field aiming for gap which lies to left of sight-line to church tower ahead. Through gap in hedge and continue in same direction now aiming for gateway with house well beyond it. Through gateway and bear diagonally right across field towards gate in hedge ahead. Through gate, bear right onto road and soon bear left at road junction near entry to small village of Littleton Drew, which has no shop or inn. *Its church has a slender Perpendicular tower and in the porch are two large pieces of a 9th-century Saxon cross.* Go straight through village passing telephone box and church on right and ignoring footpath signs.

(F) Follow road out of village, going straight, not left at road junction just beyond and soon beneath noisy M4 motorway to arrive at T-junction. Cross busy B4039 with great care and go to left of small shed, straight down narrow surfaced lane. Pass Goulter's Mill Farm on right (B & B), then bear left passing cart-shed on left before crossing bridge over By Brook *(we shall soon rejoin this stream and then follow it until flows into the Avon, just beyond Bathford - see page 46).* Bear left beyond bridge, through metal gate and soon bear right, following track up hill to right of beech plantation. Through metal gate at end of plantation and keep straight up right-hand edge of field with wall to right. Through hunting gate at top of field and keep straight along right-hand edge of field with hedge on right. *Note Lugbury Long Barrow over to left, with the great stones of its main chambered tomb exposed on its top. Described by the 17th-century antiquary, John Aubrey, as 'a great Table stone of bastard freestone leaning on two pitched perpendicular stones', it is still impressive today. Constructed in Neolithic times it must already have been over two thousand years old when the Roman legionaries were building the nearby Fosse Way.* Bear right beyond small spinney and go through two metal hunting gates. Follow to immediate right of stone wall and after veering left, through large metal gate and keep on track to immediate right of wall.

(G) Through large metal gates and turn left onto road. Follow this road and over small x-rds crossing the Fosse Way (see page 20) (SP - Nettleton). *(But turn right if you wish to visit Stables Tea Room or Fosse Farm Country Hotel - visible from here.)* Keep down sunken lane, passing golf course on left, then over ladder stile beside gate and go quietly between houses at Nettleton Mill.

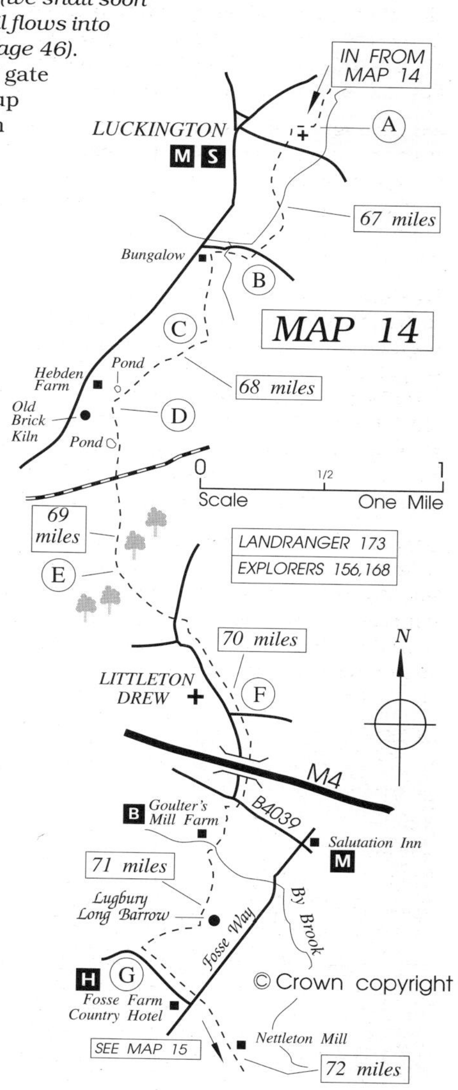

Houses near the Market Cross, Castle Combe

(A) Through concealed kissing gate to right of wrought-iron gate and bear left onto tree-shaded, surfaced path with pretty tributary stream alongside on left. Soon over stile and emerge onto golf course where we turn right and go on well surfaced path, keeping eye open for stray golf-balls and virtually silent golf-trolleys. Cross By Brook over attractive neo-Gothic stone bridge and immediately turn right keeping on well surfaced path. Manor House Hotel visible down valley to right. Soon fork left going slightly uphill, leave golf course and go up path, bearing left, with wall on right and woods up to left. Turn right through squeeze-stile and down stone steps with walls on both sides. Under small stone bridge and soon onto surfaced driveway leading into Castle Combe.

(B) Under bridged gap between two houses. *This gap frames a delightful view of the Market Cross and the many old buildings surrounding it. Castle Combe lies snugly in the wooded valley of the little By Brook, with several fine old buildings around its little Market Cross reminding us of wealth once generated here by cloth weavers. The substantial tower of the largely Perpendicular church was built in 1434 'at the expense of the clothiers of the district', and the church's interior is well worth visiting.* Pass Castle Inn on left and church over to right before bearing right by Market Cross onto busier road with White Hart Inn opposite. Pass Post Office shop on left and over attractive stone bridge crossing By Brook. *It was in 1966 that the streamside down to the left was temporarily transformed by the producers of the film* Dr Doolittle *into a tiny 'harbour' complete with boats and jetty, a move not universally popular at the time.*

(C) Beyond end of village, turn left to cross small stone bridge over By Brook and immediately bear right onto well used path (SP - *Long Dean*). Over stone stile and bear up path to left into 'Conservation Area'. Now on slope with stream down to right, trees above to left and pools soon visible to right. Along path partly overhung with trees and bushes and into woodlands - fairly muddy in wet weather. Eventually go over stile across wall by gate and over another stile before starting to descend track with entry to sewage works on right (not very apparent).

(D) Enter pretty stone hamlet of Long Dean in its quiet, wooded valley, bearing right over small bridge and right again by Nut Tree Cottage up to left. Leave hamlet on track, cross bridge over By Brook ignoring waymark to left. Bear right at end of track by last house in hamlet and up steep, sunken path through woods. Through gate at end of woods and keep on well defined path with overhanging hedge to immediate right. Good views across valley to left. At gap in bushes, where main path bears to right, fork left following well defined path across slope of field and aiming for woods at far left-hand top end. Over stile and turn left onto road. Follow this narrow sunken road **with great care** down hill through woodlands, keeping on left-hand side to be on outside of bend.

(E) Bear right onto busy A420 (SP - *Bristol*) at entry to village of Ford. Pass bus shelter on right. Almost immediately **cross A420 with care** and turn left onto minor road (SP - *Colerne*). Pass White Hart Inn on left, go straight, not left just beyond, and at end of village, beyond house called *Tredena* on right, turn left over stile. Go over field keeping fence and trees on immediate left with small stream soon joining By Brook. Now veer right keeping By Brook, with its fishermen's benches, on left. Bear left, over footbridge crossing attractive By Brook above weir and over stone stile immediately beyond. Bear left by end of weir, following path along foot of woods to left and after climbing a little, aim for gate at right-hand end of fence ahead. Through this and veer left to aim for gate in left-hand corner of field.

(F) Through metal gate, go over road at T-junction and over stile almost opposite. Go to left of Slaughterford's churchyard wall. Pass gate to churchyard on right. *The church with its pleasant tower lay derelict for nearly 200 years, having apparently been greatly damaged by Cromwell's troops when on their way to Ireland. It was rebuilt in 1883 and its interior still has a Victorian flavour. The small village just beyond lies quietly in the deep, wooded valley of the By Brook.* Go straight down to gate beyond churchyard to bear left onto pathway above road. Pass village seat and attractive cottages on left. Bear left keeping on road with By Brook now on immediate right. Bear left onto narrow road just before bridge on right (SP - *Weight limit 7.5 tonnes*). Bear right keeping on road overhung with trees (ignoring footpath and bridleway fingerposts).

(G) Straight, not left, at road junction at end of woods and onto Weavern Lane which is surfaced in its initial stages. Go straight across keeping on lane (SP - *Unsuitable for Motors)* (lane up to left leads to Honeybrook Farm). Weavern Lane now overhung with trees and often muddy. At start of Husseyhill Wood, with its attractive coppice plantations, go straight across at junction of tracks, ignoring waymark to left.

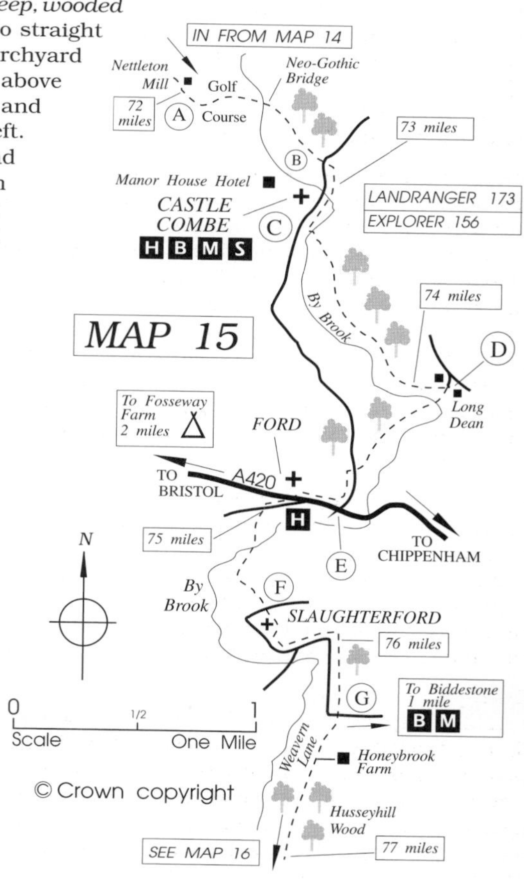

(A) After about half-a-mile turn left, keeping on track which soon becomes much narrower, with overhanging bushes. After 250 yards turn right off lane by oak trees and through metal gate. Go down narrow bridleway into more open country with hedge on right and fence on left. At end of field go down sunken path with hedge to left and fence to right. Through small wooden gate and down path with fence still on right. Cross track at end of short field, through small wooden gate and pass notice stating *'No swimming'*. Cross small stream with ruins of Weavern Farm over to right and fences on both sides of path.

(B) Over stone bridge crossing now substantial By Brook and through small wooden gate going up slope. Along path with Tilley's Wood just to right and fence to left. Pleasant views to left of By Brook and Hungerford Woods on slopes beyond. Through small wooden gate following well marked path across field with By Brook down to left and bushes and trees to right. Through small wooden gate to left of metal gate with By Brook just below to left. Go across field and eventually pass Widdenham Farmhouse on left before going over stile by large wooden gate on to surfaced driveway.

(C) Onto road passing Widdenham Farm's farmyard and cottages on right and soon go straight ahead through large metal gate where road goes to right. Cross large field following path running approximately parallel with By Brook. Through small gate with By Brook now on immediate left and through field with By Brook still on left, heading for metal gate with farmhouse just beyond.

(D) Over stile beside metal gate and bear left onto road passing Saltbox Farm on right (B&B). Bear right at road junction beyond Saltbox Farm and up slight incline before turning left to go over stile. Follow left-hand hedge for short distance, then through squeeze stile and bear right on well used path to cross large field keeping just to right of bend of By Brook. Spire of Box church visible well ahead, above waters of stream. Through squeeze stile in cross-hedge just to right of By Brook and keep beside this stream, with its rushes and ducks, passing a few gardens on slopes beyond. Over stile in fence and immediately turn right by small weir, with fence on right. Bear left, with part of now divided stream on left, onto well surfaced path. Over footbridge onto wood-chipping path and bear left over attractive arched footbridge. Now turn right with By Brook on immediate right and fence on left. Box Mill (now a theatre) over to left.

(E) Bear left with care onto road entering village of Box. *Situated above the valley of the By Brook, the substantial village of Box has a number of handsome stone houses, the great quarries here having supplied much of the stone used by the builders of its neighbour, Bath. The long Box Tunnel was one of the great features of Brunel's Great Western railway line and the south aisle of Box Church was specially built for the use of his great gang of navvies.* Pass Box Mill on left and under busy railway line before taking

Path beside the By Brook, approaching Saltbox Farm

first of two footpaths to right by going through kissing gate below transformer on pole. *(The main Macmillan Way goes along a short, surfaced roadway just beyond, and across a field up into the village, on its way to distant Abbotsbury on the Dorset coast.)* Go along narrow pathway with wire fence and railway embankment to right and small stream to left. Soon cross stone bridge over By Brook and seat down to left overlooking the river. Through wooden kissing gate and across meadow initially aiming for distant service station roof. Entry to short railway tunnel up to right beyond tree-clad bank. Below low-voltage power line veer well to right aiming for small fenced enclosure with small black and white marker in front of it. *Note far end of small railway tunnel with its handsome portal partly visible up to right.* Through large metal gate to right of fenced enclosure and through underbridge beneath railway embankment. Through metal gate into field and keep to its right-hand edge with trees to immediate right. Over stile beside large metal gate and go up surfaced roadway with semi-detached cottage to left.

(F) Cross road just to left of road junction and over stile into field. Veer slightly left to aim for fenced gap in cross-hedge, passing large house up to right. Over stile beside fenced gap with low-voltage power pole just to right and then veer right to aim for gateway near top, right-hand end of cross-hedge. Beyond gateway veer very slightly left and head for gateway in next cross-hedge. Over stile beside large metal gate in cross-hedge and head across field to pass close to By Brook which is on our left, before going through gap in scanty cross-hedge with trees. Keep in same direction going across sloping bank to aim for stile in cross-hedge well to right of By Brook. Over this double stile before crossing small tributary stream (possibly dry in mid-summer). Keep in same direction across next large field with glimpses of handsome 18th-century Shockerwick House up to right. When half-way across this field aim for point where hedge coming in from right meets wooded edge of By Brook, eventually aiming for blue signboard..

(G) Over two stiles beside bridge over By Brook with daffodils, snowdrops and a welcome seat *(The Bailiff's Seat)*. Keep in almost same direction up unsigned road to immediate left of blue signboard, with house visible ahead. Walk with care up this rather narrow road soon passing two springs on right and house called South Lodge, also on right. Climb up steadily before bearing left at road junction *(no sign our direction)* onto slightly wider road .

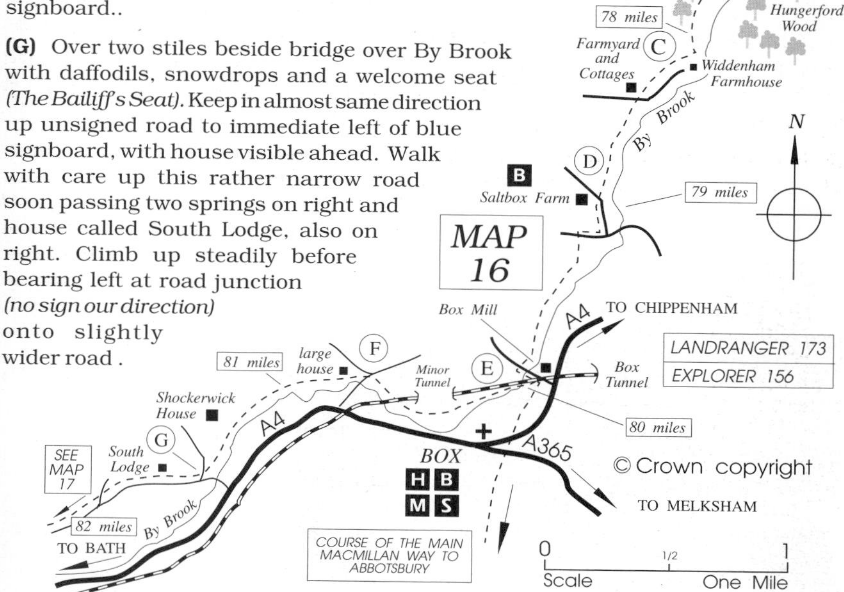

(A) Ignore footpath up to right, near 'Europump Kiosk' on left, but after about 200 yards turn left over stone stile beside metal gate. Go down field following first wall and then hedge, both to immediate right. Soon on to partly surfaced track. Bathford church tower visible across valley slightly to left. Through gateway below power line and soon turn right immediately before reaching wooden shed. Walk in front of this and then turn left to continue downwards with hedge again to immediate right. Go over stile and continue down field with hedge still to immediate right. Over stile to right of two houses and down short track before turning right onto footway beside the ever-busy A4 road.

The Roman Baths, Bath

(B) Pass first part of Bathford Nurseries on immediate right but **well before** end of this establishment turn left and **cross A4 with great care** to go down track leading through underbridge below railway embankment. Keep straight up path passing paper mill on right and crossing By Brook. Over stile and continue in same direction up field. Through narrow iron squeeze stile with garden wall to right and up narrow path with hedges on both sides. Through stone squeeze stile and turn right on to public road at entry to Bathford village. Pass elegant Whitehaven House on right and soon turn down right at X-rds by telephone box *(no sign). Distant view of earthworks of Little Solisbury Iron Age hillfort ahead across valley.* Pass entrance drive to paper mill down to right. Pass Lodge Hotel and Crown Inn, both on left, and ---

(C) --- Bear right on to busy A363, keeping to footway. Over bridge crossing By Brook and **cross to opposite side of road with great care**, with car parking area on left. Just before reaching railway underbridge turn left off road through gap in wall and soon fork right to go up path gradually climbing railway embankment. At top of embankment go between bridge parapet on left and fenced-off railway lines on right. *Hold on to your hat if you hear a train coming your way - they move **very** fast!* Look over parapet to see the place where the By Brook flows into the River Avon - our final farewell to a stream that has kept us company since Goulter's Mill, north of Castle Combe, a distance of about 12 miles. Having crossed the River Avon, bear left down embankment and go over stile to left. Now head diagonally right across large, flat field aiming for stile in fenceline ahead. Over stile at T-junction of fences and keep in same direction aiming for left-hand end of long stone house. Over stile and up concrete steps in embankment before crossing railway line **with great care**, observing the sign stating - STOP, LOOK, LISTEN. Over stile just beyond railway and go up lane passing to immediate right of low stone house. Bathampton church visible ahead.

(D) Immediately beyond house on left, turn left to go through gap in fence and turn right to join towpath beside the Kennet and Avon Canal. *This towpath is the final part of the 84-mile-long Kennet and Avon National Waterway Walk which runs from Reading to Bath.* Soon go under bridge No 183 and pass the attractive George Inn on right. *(We shall now keep on this pleasant towpath for just over two miles.)* Now running parallel with the main railway line into Bath. Go under bridge No 184. A welcome bench just beyond. First signs of Georgian Bath visible over to right and then past a number of 'long-term' moored narrow boats, not all as bright and cheerful as we had expected. Pass footbridge No 185 to our left.

(E) Under short stone-lined tunnel with attractive portal at its far end. Under two graceful iron bridges both dated *Anno 1800* passing small public park on right. Canal banks are now stoned-lined and most attractive. Go through second tunnel, this one with handsome portals at each end and an impressive Georgian house above it. Beyond tunnel, bear right and right again to cross head of tunnel and bear right yet again to join towpath now on left-hand side of canal. Pass 'The Moorings' development on opposite side of canal. Go up sloping path and cross busy public road with great care before turning right to cross canal bridge in Bathwick. Immediately beyond bridge turn left to go down steps to towpath, which is now on right-hand side of canal again. Now passing more moored boats and Bath Abbey at last visible over to right.

(F) Just before reaching lock turn right down steep path with some steps (Sign - *Toilets*). Cross minor road by entry to school on right and continue in same direction on surfaced footpath. Go through tall underbridge beneath railway embankment, turn left and almost immediately right to cross busy road on a controlled crossing. Veer slightly right to pass in front of toilets and bear left down North Parade. Pass car park on left (Bath Cricket Club). Cross to opposite side of road with care as soon as possible. Continue in same direction and cross River Avon, with good view of Pulteney Bridge up to right. Turn right at traffic lights and go along pavement with park below to right. Turn left at controlled traffic lights and go straight ahead to pass to left-hand side of Bath Abbey. Turn right at end of Abbey to enter by its small west door, thus completing your journey down the Cross-Cotswold Pathway.

The Cotswold Way starts its journey northwards from here - But perhaps you will feel like an hour or two's well-earned rest, before setting out! On a more serious note - Congratulations on completing the Cross-Cotswold Pathway. We do hope that you have enjoyed it.

It is impossible to do justice to Bath in a few lines, and we suggest that, having drawn breath, you call at the very helpful Tourist Information Centre which is close to the Abbey. Whatever else you decide to do, make sure to visit the splendidly vaulted Abbey, the nearby Roman Baths, the Museum of Costume in the Assembly Rooms and the spacious riverside below Pulteney Bridge.

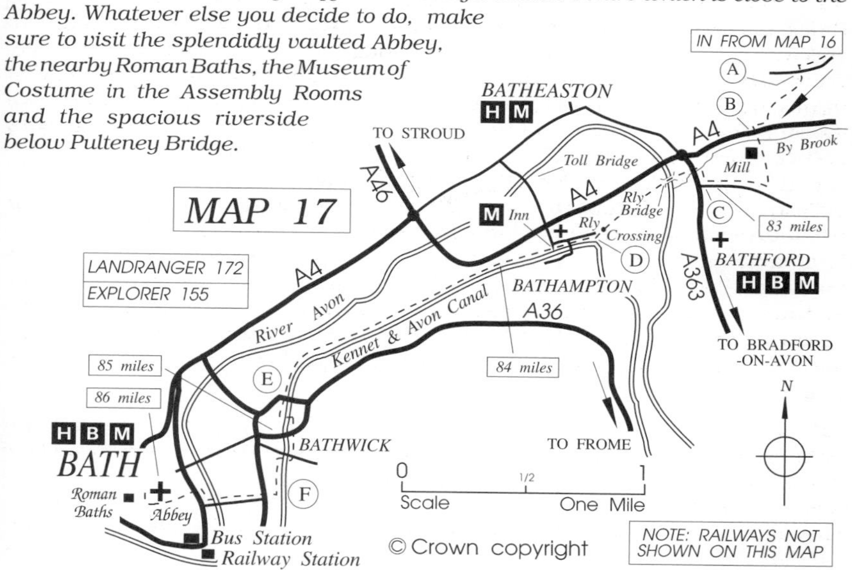

INDEX

WALK ACROSS THE COTSWOLDS AND SUPPORT MACMILLAN

If you would like to help raise funds for Macmillan Cancer Relief, could you ask a few of your friends, relations and colleagues at work to sponsor your walk. If you dont feel like doing this, perhaps you would consider 'sponsoring' yourself - any contributions would be most gratefully received. All cheques should be made payable to Macmillan Cancer Relief and they should be forwarded to the Macmillan Way Association at St Mary's Barn, Pillerton Priors, Warwick CV35 0PG. They will then be forwarded to Macmillan Cancer Relief. Should you wish it a Certificate of Achievement and Thanks could be forwarded to you.

If you would like us to send you an A4-size Sponsor Form with a heading similar to the example but with more space below for sponsors' names and amounts, do drop us a line.

THE CROSS-COTSWOLD PATHWAY SPONSORSHIP FORM

Issued by the Macmillan Way Association - An independent organisation supporting Macmillan Cancer Relief - Registered Charity Number 261017

Fighting cancer with more than medicine

I/We______________________(name)______________________ ______________________(address) __________(post code) are planning to walk a section of the Cross-Cotswold Pathway / The Cotswold Link / The Cotswold Round and we would be most grateful if you would sponsor us to help raise funds for Macmillan Cancer Relief. We are hoping to walk from______________ to______________, a distance of about ______ miles. If you feel that this venture is worth sponsoring, could you write in the appropriate columns below, indicating how many pence per mile you would be prepared to donate. I/We will let you know how we fared. Macmillan Cancer Relief is directed towards improving the care and support available to people with cancer and their families. If you can help it would be much appreciated.

NAME	INITIALS	ADDRESS	AMOUNT PER MILE		